# COLONIALISM AND THE REVOLUTIONARY PERIOD

## (BEGINNINGS–1800)

**Jerry Phillips, Ph.D.**
*General Editor to First Edition*

Department of English
University of Connecticut, Storrs

**Michael Anesko, Ph.D.**
*Adviser and Contributor*

Director, Honors Program in English
Pennsylvania State University

**Karen Meyers, Ph.D.**
*Principal Author*

CHELSEA HOUSE PUBLISHERS
An imprint of Infobase Publishing

**Colonialism and the Revolutionary Period (Beginnings–1800)**



**DEVELOPED AND PRODUCED FOR CHELSEA HOUSE BY DWJ BOOKS LLC**



Chelsea House
An imprint of Infobase Publishing
132 West 31st Street
New York NY 10001

**Library of Congress Cataloging-in-Publication Data**

Meyers, Karen, 1948-
Colonialism and the revolutionary period : beginnings to 1800 / Jerry Phillips, general editor; Michael Anesko, adviser and contributor; Karen Meyers, principal author.—2nd ed.
p. cm.—(Backgrounds to American literature)
Includes bibliographical references and index.

ISBN 978-1-60413-485-8 (hardcover : alk. paper)

1. American literature—Colonial period, ca. 1600–1775—History and criticism. 2. American literature—Revolutionary period, 1775–1783—History and criticism. 3. United States—History—Revolution, 1775–1783—Literature and the revolution. 4. Revolutionary literature, American—History and criticism. 5. American literature—1783–1850—History and criticism. 6. United States—Intellectual life—17th century. 7. United States—Intellectual life—18th century. 8. Imperialism in literature. 9. Colonies in literature. I. Phillips, Jerry (Jerry R.) II. Anesko, Michael. III. Title. IV. Series.
PS185.M49 2010
810.9'001–dc22 2009029629

Chelsea House books are available at special discounts when purchased in bulk quantities for businesses, associations, institutions, or sales promotions. Please call our Special Sales Department in New York at (212) 967-8800 or (800) 322-8755.

You can find Chelsea House on the World Wide Web at http://www.chelseahouse.com

Text design by DWJ BOOKS LLC
Cover printed by Bang Printing, Brainerd, MN
Book printed and bound by Bang Printing, Brainerd, MN
Date printed: April 2010
Printed in the United States of America

**Acknowledgments**
pp. 11, 15, 27, 39, 43, 51, 65, 71, 77: Library of Congress, Prints and Photographs Division
p. 21: North Wind Pictures
pp. 89, 93: The Granger Collection, New York

10 9 8 7 6 5 4 3 2 1

This book is printed on acid-free paper.

All links and Web addresses were checked and verified to be correct at the time of publication. Because of the dynamic nature of the Web, some addresses and links may have changed since publication and may no longer be valid.

# Contents

# Preface

The five volumes of *Backgrounds to American Literature* explore 500 years of American literature by looking at the times during which the literature developed. Through a period's historical antecedents and characteristics—political, cultural, religious, economic, and social—each chapter covers a specific period, theme, or genre.

In this new edition of the series, a final chapter looks at the period through another lens—that of the women who lived and worked in colonial and revolutionary America, women whose voices have been little heard. Through their diaries and letters, readers will gain another perspective on the new land and its peoples. In addition to these seven chapters, readers will find a useful timeline of drama and theatrical history, poetry and prose, and history; a glossary of terms (also identified by SMALL CAPITAL LETTERS throughout the text); a biographical glossary; suggestions for further reading; and an index. By helping readers explore literature in the context of human history, the editors hope to encourage readers to further explore the literary world.

# 1. The First 300 Years

From the "discovery" of America in the fifteenth century to the beginning of the nineteenth century, the world changed from one dominated by religious belief to one shaped by scientific knowledge; governments evolved from absolute monarchies to democracies; and men and women began to think of themselves in a new and different way, not as peasants attached to the land of a lord but as free people with the right to self-determination.

American literature, as it developed over the first 300 years, was influenced by a number of factors. Certainly, like America itself, American literature is a "melting pot," a complex fusion of the native cultures of the original settlers and the many groups of immigrants who populated the new land. It was also influenced by the very existence of the wilderness, vast stretches of land, populated by Native American peoples who were alternately inspiring and frightening. The first settlers in New England brought with them an intense religious belief and a piety that has seldom been equaled in religious history, along with ideas about morality and conduct that permanently affected how Americans think and feel and how

American writers write. Enlightenment philosophy, imported from Europe, took root in America and grew to shape its founding documents and spur a revolution that changed the world. From this sea of change came a literature of revolution and rights—and a new mythology, a new vision of what a human could be and do.

## Native Americans and Colonial Visions of a New World

When the first white settlers arrived in America, they encountered a diverse group of peoples they called "Indians," so named by Christopher Columbus because he believed he had circumnavigated the globe and landed in India. Today, the term *Indian* is regarded as degrading; it is not only incorrect but it also ignores the fact that these peoples were the original owners of the land and the fact that they were an extraordinarily diverse group with different languages and cultures.

Some European settlers, particularly the French, established close, respectful relationships with the native tribes they encountered. For a number of reasons, however, the relationship between Native Americans and the English settlers was quite different. Many of those who first arrived on the shores of the so-called "New World" held religious beliefs that led them to categorize non-Christians as barbarians or "savages." Initially, many colonists, including the French, believed that it was important to convert the native people. Although the French were able to convert many Native Americans to Roman Catholicism, the English colonists were less successful. They began to regard the native people as "devils" or "animals," and the colonists saw their task as one of clearing the "howling wilderness," which meant getting rid of the people as well as the trees.

The impact of these negative STEREOTYPES of Native Americans on American history and literature are many and complex. One important consequence is that, for many years, educators taught American literature as if it began in 1492, when Columbus "discovered" America, ignoring the myths and legends of the native people. Because most Native American cultures did not have written languages, it was easy to disregard this large body of oral literature. Another important consequence of these negative stereotypes is an obsession with the idea of the wilderness that permeates American literature. The forest was regarded as a frightening place, the home of Satan and of the evil savage. Still, as much as many colonists were afraid of the wilderness, they were also fascinated by it. Like Adam and Eve forbidden the apple, many deeply religious Puritans were powerfully drawn to the wilderness, even though they felt it to be evil. This tension between the wilderness as symbolic of the Garden of Eden and the wilderness as symbolic of savagery and temptation colors many works of American literature from the earliest histories and sermons to contemporary fiction. Allied with the idea of the wilderness is that of the Native American, who, at times, is regarded as the "noble savage," the very ideal of a human being free from the corrupting influence of urban life, and who, at other times, is seen as the very devil—the epitome of the "heart of darkness," the evil that may lie deep in the souls of even the best of humans.

## Traditional Native American Literature

One of the first characteristics one notices in reading Native American myths and legends is the deep and abiding respect for the natural world felt by native peoples. Although Native Americans hunted buffalo and farmed the land, they did so with a quite different attitude than that of the European colonists. Many Native American myths and legends emphasize the duty of the people to take care of the land, to thank the slain buffalo for the gift of his life, and to take only what is needed from nature—never more. Native American poetry, much of which is religious in nature, expresses this same reverence for the earth and its gifts, this same sense of unity with nature. The title poem of a collection of Native American poetry, for example, tells us, with the brevity and vividness of a HAIKU, "Earth always endures." Another poem from the Yokuts people begins, "My words are tied in one / With the great mountains," and the speaker of the poem goes on to ask the mountains, rocks, and trees to help him "with your supernatural power."

From such a perspective, it is easy to see why Native Americans were initially so confused by the attitudes and behavior of the European colonists. Because many Native Americans had no concept of *owning* land—land was, rather, on loan from a higher power—they could not have comprehended what it meant to sell it when the colonists offered to buy.

Over the years, Native American myths and legends began to include references to white people, many of which are quite unflattering. In a Cheyenne myth, for example, the GREAT SPIRIT creates animals, "who had hair all over their bodies," white men, "who had hair all over their heads and faces and on their legs," and red men, "who had very long hair on their heads only." The white men "were in a class with the wolf, for both were the trickiest and most cunning creatures in that beautiful world." In a Yuma myth,

### Native American Religious Beliefs

**It is important to remember that Native American mythology, unlike Greek mythology, reflects a living religion that is still practiced today. In that sense, Native American myths are more akin to the Bible than they are to stories of Zeus on Mount Olympus. In fact, there are many similarities between Native American religions and Christianity. For example, Native American creation myths share elements of the biblical story of Genesis, in which a supreme being creates the universe and all its creatures out of nothingness. Several Native American tribes also have stories that closely parallel that of Noah's ark, in which a flood destroys the earth and one good person is chosen to save his family and two of each animal species.**

**However, there are also very significant differences between Native American religions and Christianity, the most important of which is the fact that Native Americans do not make a sharp distinction between the natural and supernatural. Whereas Christians tend to emphasize the vast difference between the material world and the spiritual realm, Native Americans tend to regard plants, animals, and people as sharing in the divinity of the creator.**

**Thus, Native American spirituality is inextricably linked with a respect for all of nature. According to storyteller Jenny Leading Cloud, Native Americans**

> ***think of the earth and the whole universe as a never-ending circle, and in this circle man is just another animal. The buffalo and the coyote are our brothers; the birds, our cousins. Even the tiniest ant, even a louse, even the smallest flower you can find—they are all relatives. We end our prayers with the words mitakuye oyasin—"all my relations"—and that includes everything that grows, crawls, runs, creeps, hops, and flies on this continent. White people see man as nature's master and conqueror, but [we] . . . who are close to nature, know better. [Erdoes, p. 5]***

"The white man . . . [cries] because his hair was faded and curly and his skin pale and washed out. The white man was always pouting and selfish. Whatever he saw, he had to have at once. He had been created childish and greedy." In a Pima myth, the Magician who made the world decides to bake himself some creatures in an oven. Some of them—the Native Americans—come out perfectly, "neither underdone nor overdone." However, some were undercooked, "not brown enough"; these, the Magician exiles. "They don't belong here—they belong across the water someplace." With very different worldviews and values, Native Americans and whites seemed destined to be at odds with one another.

## O Brave New World

William Shakespeare's (1564–1616) play *The Tempest* (1611) is set in Bermuda, in what was then called "the new world." When the play's hero, Prospero, and his daughter, Miranda, are shipwrecked there, Miranda exclaims, "O, wonder! / How many goodly creatures are there here! / How beauteous mankind is! O brave new world / That has such people in it!" However, this new world already has an occupant that Miranda has not yet met, Caliban, a "savage and deformed slave." Thus, Shakespeare's play reflects both the longing for a new beginning and the fear of the unknown that many explorers and colonists felt about the Americas.

Writing to King Ferdinand and Queen Isabella of Spain, Christopher Columbus (1451–1506) describes the beauty and riches of the islands he discovers:

> **There are mountains of very great size and beauty, vast plains, groves, and very fruitful fields, admirably adapted for tillage, pasture, and habitation. The convenience and excellence of the harbors in this island, and the abundance of the rivers, so indispensable to the health of man, surpass anything that would be believed by one who has not seen it.**

He portrays the native people as childlike and fearful, noting that they go about "naked as they were born," and "give objects of great value for trifles," adding that they "bartered, like idiots, cotton and gold for fragments of bows, glasses, bottles, and jars; which I forbad as being unjust, and myself gave them many beautiful and acceptable articles which I had brought with me." Columbus's reason for attempting to treat the natives fairly was not an ideal of justice but rather an attempt "to conciliate them, that they might be led to become Christians, and be inclined to entertain a regard for the King and Queen . . . and that I might induce them to take an interest in seeking out, and collecting and delivering to us things as they possessed in abundance, but which we greatly needed." Columbus's attitude toward the natives makes abundantly clear the profound differences between Native American and European worldviews. Columbus sees the land and its riches as commodities,

### ▪ ▪ ▪ ▪ CALIBAN ▪ ▪ ▪ ▪

Critics of Shakespeare's *The Tempest* have regarded the monstrous Caliban as the opposite of the play's hero, Prospero. Prospero seems to personify art and imagination, whereas Caliban appears to represent all of humanity's more beastlike characteristics. Because *The Tempest* is based on the true story of a shipwreck in the Bermudas, Caliban, a native of the island, would appear to be Shakespeare's version of a "Native American." As such, his portrait is ambiguous. Along with Caliban's drinking, swearing, and petty plotting, Shakespeare also portrays his love of the natural beauty of the island. Sounding much like the Native Americans who initially helped the settlers only to be betrayed by them, Caliban tells Prospero,

*This Island's mine . . .*
*Which thou tak'st from me.*
*When thou camest first,*
*Thou strok'dst me and mad'st much of me . . . and then I loved thee*
*And show'd thee all the qualities o' the isle,*
*The fresh springs, brine-pits, barren place and fertile.*

Later, sounding as lyrical as any poet, Caliban speaks of his love of the place and its myriad sounds:

*The isle is full of noises,*
*Sounds and sweet airs, that give delight and hurt not.*
*Sometimes a thousand twangling instruments*
*Will hum about mine ears, and sometime voices*
*That, if I then had waked after long sleep,*
*Will make me sleep again: and then, in dreaming,*
*The clouds methought would open and show riches*
*Ready to drop upon me that, when I waked,*
*I cried to dream again.*

William M. Hamlin in *The Image of America in Montaigne, Spenser, and Shakespeare: Renaissance Ethnography and Literary Reflection* speculates that the ambiguous nature of Caliban's character reflects a "genuine uncertainty regarding the human status of cultural aliens."

That is, many Europeans at the time could not decide if Native Americans were mere savages, little better than animals, or examples of humankind in its natural state.

items to be used up to satisfy human wants and needs, whereas the Taino—the native tribe that first greeted him and whose name means "good" or "noble"—have virtually no sense of owning anything, certainly not the land itself.

Intentionally or not, Columbus and his fellow explorers brought disaster to the people of the islands. A Spanish priest, Bartolome de las Casas (1484–1566), who accompanied Columbus on his third voyage, estimated that more than three million natives in Cuba alone died as a direct result of the Spanish colonization between 1494 and 1508.

## The Virgin Land

Although later colonists would settle in America in order to escape religious persecution, the earliest English visitors, such as those at Jamestown in what is now Virginia, came to find gold and other riches, which they intended to send back to England. Prominent among this group was Captain John Smith (1580–1631), whose *True Relation of Such Occurrences and Accidents of Note as Hath Happened in Virginia since the First Planting of that Colony* (1608) is the first printed American book. This work and others that Smith wrote in later years were designed to encourage Europeans to come to America. Often criticized for boastfulness and not above tinkering with the truth to make a better story, Smith nevertheless had a tremendous impact on how the New World was perceived by the Old. It is important to note that the colony of Virginia, named after Elizabeth I (1558–1603) of England, who chose, she said, to remain a virgin in order to devote herself completely to her subjects, was as much an idea as a place. It was "virgin land" to the colonists. Ignoring the fact that it was already inhabited, they saw it as a symbol of limitless untapped wealth, fruit ripe for the picking.

Smith and a group of adventurers arrived in what is now Virginia in 1607; his adventures in Virginia ended in 1609, when a spark ignited his powder bag and he was severely burned. He returned to England to recover but returned to America in 1614, where for six months he explored the coasts of Massachusetts and Maine. Although he is often associated with Virginia, Smith's writings about the land he called "New England" were designed to encourage settlers to try their luck in this rich land:

> **The Isles of Mattahunts are on the West side of this Bay, where are many Isles, and questionless good harbors; and then the Country of the Massachusetts, which is the Paradise of all those**

**The First Thanksgiving**

This impression of the first Thanksgiving was painted between 1900 and 1920 by Philadelphia artist Jean Louis Gerome Ferris. The actual feast was three days long, and some 90 Native Americans, along with the Pilgrims, ate venison, wild turkeys, and, perhaps, pumpkin—though not in pie form.

The Pilgrims' feast was not, as many people think, the beginning of an annual tradition; rather, it was a one-time celebration of a good harvest. President Abraham Lincoln established the annual Thanksgiving celebration by proclamation in 1863.

### THE TRUE STORY OF POCAHONTAS

Every American knows the story of Captain John Smith whose life was saved by Chief Powhatan's daughter, Pocahontas. In December 1607, according to Smith, he was captured and taken to the home of Powhatan. He was at first welcomed by the chief but was subsequently forced to lie on two flat stones while male members of the tribe stood over him with clubs. Smith assumed he was to be beaten to death but tells his readers he was saved when Powhatan's daughter Pocahontas lay her body over his: She "hazarded the beating out of her own braines to save mine, and not only that, but so prevailed upon her father that I was safely conveyed to Jamestown."

Many scholars and historians have questioned the accuracy of this story. For one thing, Smith's original narration of his captivity did not include it, and Smith first recorded the story only after Pocahontas had come to England with her husband, John Rolfe. Introduced to the royal family, she was something of a celebrity; thus, some historians speculate that Smith merely wanted to enhance his own reputation. Other scholars do not doubt the story but are convinced that Smith misunderstood what was happening. It may have been that Smith was thrown on the rocks as part of a ritual ceremony, and Pocahontas's role was to pretend to save him.

Perhaps more important than the story's historical truth is the fact that it was repeated until it gained the status of a legend. Pocahontas's willingness to sacrifice herself for Smith seems to symbolize the idea that Native Americans in general ought to give in to the invaders. In many cultures, the stories that are most often repeated reveal not history but the wishes and dreams of the people. And early English settlers certainly wished and hoped that Native Americans would yield peacefully to their supposedly "superior" culture and sacrifice their claim to the land and natural resources.

> parts; for, here are many Isles all planted with corn; groves, mulberries, savage gardens, and good harbors; the Coast is for the most part, high clayey sandy cliffs. As you pass along the Sea Coast, you see all along large corn fields.

Smith was a practical man who generally got along well with the Native Americans he met, but his attitude toward the land makes it clear that he sees all of it as ripe for the taking. The "savage" gardens and cornfields are the prizes he dangles before the eyes of prospective colonists.

## "A Hideous and Desolate Wilderness"

The Pilgrims who arrived at Plymouth Rock on the Mayflower in 1620 came to America for reasons quite different from those that motivated the colonists at Jamestown in Virginia. These settlers, like the later Puritan settlers of the Massachusetts Bay Colony, left Europe because of religious persecution. The Pilgrims, so called by William Bradford (1590–1657), later governor of Plymouth Colony, were SEPARATISTS. In his *Of Plymouth Plantation,* written between 1630 and 1650 but not published until 1856, Bradford explains why the Pilgrims originally chose to come to America. He says that "the hardness of the place and country" appealed to the Pilgrims because "few in comparison would come to them, and fewer that would bide it out and continue with them." That is, the separatists, tired of religious disputes, wanted a forbidding place so that only like-minded people would join them, people willing to sacrifice everything in order to be able to practice their religion as they chose. When the Pilgrims arrived in America, they found that it was every bit as wild and forbidding as they might have hoped. According to Bradford, they could see nothing but

> **a hideous and desolate wilderness, full of wild beasts and wild men—and what multitudes there might be of them they knew not. Neither could they, as it were, go up to the top of Pisgah [the mountain from which Moses saw Canaan, the "Promised Land"] to view from this wilderness a more goodly country to feed their hopes; for which way soever they turned their eyes (save upward to the heavens) they could have little solace or content in respect of any outward objects.**

However, Bradford says, the Pilgrims "cried unto the Lord, and He heard their voice and looked on their adversity." It is important to note that Bradford, writing some years after the settlement of the colony, is not simply writing a history; he is also attempting to instill in the children and grandchildren of the original Pilgrims the same faith and dependence on God that their ancestors possessed.

Thus, Bradford and the Pilgrims viewed the land and people of the "new world" as a CRUCIBLE. The Pilgrims tested themselves against the harshness of the American wilderness in the hopes of finding spiritual riches. Still, they did not seek to preserve the wilderness and its "savage" inhabitants but eventually to eliminate them, despite the peaceful picture of the relationship between the Pilgrims and Native Americans portrayed in stories of the first Thanksgiving.

## City upon a Hill

The Puritan view of the "New World" bore some similarity to that of the separatists. Like the separatists, Puritans left Europe for the freedom to practice their religion. However, the Puritan leaders who guided settlers to the Massachusetts Bay Colony in 1629 also believed that they had a chance to establish an entirely new kind of society, based on religious principles, that would prepare the way for the second coming of Christ and the end of the world. Some Puritans thought the end was near, others believed it would be in the distant future, but most agreed that the "triumph of the true church on earth" would precede the end. Thus, John Winthrop (1606–1676), governor of the Massachusetts Bay Colony, which adjoined the separatist settlement at Plymouth, outlined the Puritan vision for America in *A Model of Christian Charity* (1630):

> **the Lord will be our God and delight to dwell among us, as his own people and will command a blessing upon us in all our ways, so that we shall see much more of His wisdom, power, goodness, and truth than formerly we have been acquainted with, we shall find that the God of Israel is among us . . . [and] that men shall say of succeeding plantations [settlements]: the Lord make it like that of New England: for we must Consider that we shall be as a City upon a Hill, the eyes of all people are upon us.**

Unlike the separatists, who originally wanted to live in seclusion, the Puritans viewed their journey as a very public experiment in THEOCRACY. They viewed the wilderness as dangerous and filled with savage peoples, but they believed it was their duty to clear the land and create a paradise, a Garden of Eden or a New Jerusalem. Like the Jews of the Old Testament, they were God's chosen people, they believed, whose duty was to prevail. They were never naïve enough to believe that human beings were immune from sin in the New World, but they believed they had the opportunity to establish a church that would serve as the model for congregations in England.

**Signing of the Mayflower Compact**

This agreement was signed on November 11, 1620, by the 41 men aboard the *Mayflower* while it was at anchor in Cape Cod Harbor. The Mayflower Compact asserts that a legitimate government can only be formed by the consent of those governed.

Interestingly, one of the most important documents in American history was written only because the *Mayflower* ended up many miles north of its intended destination. The Pilgrims had a royal charter to settle along the Hudson River in what is now New York state, but the ship was blown off course. Because they were planning to build a settlement that was not covered by their charter, they realized that they needed to develop their own agreement to ensure the rule of law in the colony. William Bradford, pictured here, was one of the framers of the Compact; he was unanimously selected governor of the New World shortly after the drafting of the Compact and was reelected 30 times.

### A Lively Resemblance of Hell

There exists a uniquely Puritan literary form called the "captivity narrative"; it is the story of a white person, often a woman, who was held captive by Native Americans. Although similar narratives have been written by people who were not of the Puritan faith, the origins of this GENRE remain firmly Puritan. Puritans, because of certain of their religious beliefs, believed that both good and bad fortune came into human lives directly from God, and, as such, should be interpreted as signs. Good fortune was easy to understand as God's blessing, but devout people felt a deep compulsion to understand misfortune as a sign of some improvement they or their communities were being asked to make. Thus, captivity narratives were, in some measure, religious tracts in which devout Puritans showed their neighbors that they saw God's will in their captivities.

The most famous of the captivity narratives is that of Mary Rowlandson, who was captured by Narragansetts in 1676. Of all of the captivities of women, Rowlandson's is the only one that was written by the captive herself. Thus, her story is more detailed and lively than many of the others, which were often written by ministers and which read like sermons. Although Rowlandson is always conscious to praise God for helping her through her ordeal and to show she correctly understood the meaning of what was happening to her, only in her story can we read about a mother's grief as she stumbles after her captors, carrying her dying daughter. Rowlandson's attitude toward her captors is typical of that of many settlers. She calls them "merciless heathen," "murderous wretches," and "barbarous creatures." However, as she travels with her captors, she also begins to glimpse their essential humanity as well. "One bitter cold day," she writes, "I could find no room to sit down before the fire. I went out, and could not tell what to do, but I went in to another wigwam, where they were also sitting round the fire, but the squaw laid a skin for me, and bid me sit down, and gave me some ground nuts, and bade me come again."

Although the Puritans hoped to convert the native peoples to Christianity, they regarded the unconverted as savages and had few scruples about appropriating the native people's land because the natives had, in the Puritan view, "done nothing with it." Late in the seventeenth century, clergyman Solomon Stoddard worried, "Did we wrong the Indians by buying their land at a small price?" but concluded, "we came to their market and gave them their price."

## Roger Williams (1603–1683)

Roger Williams, a Puritan clergyman who was banished from Massachusetts for holding views that were unacceptable to the leadership of the colony, had much greater respect for Native Americans and their culture than did most of his fellow settlers. Although he originally came to America "longing after natives' souls," that is, hoping to convert Native Americans, he eventually came to believe that acceptance of their beliefs was preferable to trying to change them. He was a quick and adept student of languages and eventually learned many native tongues. One of Williams's most famous works, in fact, was a book on Native American languages, *Key into the Languages of America* (1643). As he learned the native languages, Williams found himself taking the native point of view. Among the opinions Williams expressed that got him into trouble with his fellow Puritans was the idea that settlers could not claim to own any land for which they did not pay a fair price; he also argued for the right of the native people to practice their own religion, which in some ways he found preferable—at least in practice—to that of many Christians. Of the generosity of Native Americans, Williams wrote:

> I've known them to leave their house and mat
>     To lodge a friend or stranger
> When Jews and Christians oft have sent
>     Jesus Christ to the manger.

In 1636, banished for life from Massachusetts, Williams founded the colony of Rhode Island, where true religious freedom was allowed—even for Native Americans. In fact, it is to Williams, not to our Puritan forebears, that Americans owe the ideas of freedom of religion and separation of church and state.

**Religious Freedom?**

**It is a mistake to say that the Puritans came to America seeking "religious freedom" in the sense that term is used today. The Puritans did not believe that each person was free to believe what he or she wished. Quite the contrary, they were certain that people who did not share their beliefs were damned—and they did not tolerate the presence of people of different faiths. For example, between 1559 and 1661 four Quakers were hanged in Massachusetts, including a woman named Mary Dyer, who was four times banished from the colony but who repeatedly returned and attempted to convert the populace.**

# 2. The Literature of Puritanism

To understand the literature of Puritanism—indeed to understand much of American literature in general—one must understand the beliefs of the 20,000 PURITANS who settled in what is now called Massachusetts between 1620 and 1640, a period called "the GREAT MIGRATION." Many of the qualities popularly associated with Americans—such as "independence," "self-reliance," and "the Protestant work ethic"—are direct inheritances from this small group of settlers.

## Basic Religious Beliefs

The most important distinguishing feature of the Puritan settlers was their religion. Puritans were members of the Protestant Church of England who wanted to "purify" it of any vestiges of Roman Catholicism, such as priests' fancy vestments, ornate churches, incense, music, elaborate rituals, and so on. Puritans were CONGREGATIONALISTS; they believed that each congregation must be self-governing. Congregationalism is an important aspect of the PROTESTANT REFORMATION. Among the things early Protestants, including the Puritans, disliked about Catholicism was the idea that priests and other representatives of the Church hierarchy mediated, or transmitted information, between the individual and God. Protestants believed, instead, in direct relationships between individuals and God. This idea is of profound importance because once it is acknowledged that a lowly peasant, for example, can approach God independently without the mediation of a priest, it is not far to the evolution of ideas such as individualism, equality, and democracy.

## The Puritan Mind

Puritans were not only Congregationalists, they were also CALVINISTS; they believed in the five central TENETS set forth by the sixteenth-century religious reformer John Calvin. These tenets are often taught to schoolchildren with the help of a MNEMONIC aid. Each letter of the word *TULIP* stands for one of the tenets of Calvinism. They are

- **T**otal Depravity—the idea that humankind, as a result of the sin of Adam and Eve, has been completely corrupted by sin.
- **U**nconditional Election—also called Predestination—the idea that from the beginning of time God has decided which

### ▪ ▪ ▪ ▪ The Triumph of an Idea ▪ ▪ ▪ ▪

**Alexis de Tocqueville (1805–1859), in *Democracy in America* (1835) describes clearly the special character of America's Puritan settlers:**

> ***The settlers who established themselves on the shores of New England all belonged to the more independent classes of their native country. Their union on the soil of America at once presented the singular phenomenon of a society containing neither lords nor common people, neither rich nor poor. These men possessed, in proportion to their number, a greater mass of intelligence than is to be found in any European nation of our own time. All, without a single exception, had received a good education, and many of them were known in Europe for their talents and their acquirements. The other colonies had been founded by adventurers without family; the emigrants of New England brought with them the best elements of order and morality—they landed in the desert accompanied by their wives and children. But what most especially distinguished them was the aim of their undertaking. They had not been obliged by necessity to leave their country; the social position they abandoned was one to be regretted, and their means of subsistence were certain. Nor did they cross the Atlantic to improve their situation or to increase their wealth; the call which summoned them from the comforts of their homes was purely intellectual; and in facing the inevitable sufferings of exile their object was the triumph of an idea.***

humans will be saved and which condemned to damnation. Those who will be saved—called the ELECT or the SAINTS—are selected merely by the whim of God and for no other reason. Nothing the individual did or can do will influence God's choice.

- **L**imited Atonement—The idea that Christ's death on the cross atoned only for the Elect, not for all sinners.
- **I**rresistible Grace—the idea that when God—in the person of the Holy Spirit—calls to a member of the Elect, that person cannot resist the grace that is offered. Though the person may continue to sin, he or she will be continually drawn by grace to a complete conversion.
- **P**erseverance of the Saints—the idea that those who are saved are saved forever and cannot be lost.

It is easy to see that belief in these doctrines might lead to certain common character traits and behaviors among those who held them.

For example, people who constantly wondered if they were Saints intended for heaven or sinners condemned to an eternity in Hell would probably spend a lot of time in INTROSPECTION. Although Puritans did not believe that good behavior could lead to election, they did believe that election would eventually lead to good behavior. That is, a Saint will never be perfect—because of total depravity—but a Saint will keep trying to be a better person. When Benjamin Franklin (1706–1790) describes his plan for self-improvement in his *Autobiography* (1867)—including the thirteen virtues he hopes to develop in himself—he is not merely writing the first American self-help book and a prescription for all the self-made people who will follow his lead, he is also reflecting America's Puritan roots. A successful life—including wealth—was perceived as a sign of election. People who were afflicted with poverty and bad luck in life might well fear that they were not members of the elect, whereas those who prospered financially might well believe that they were among the chosen. Puritans, then, tended to overvalue material possessions—their own and those of their neighbors—and to see them as signs of moral superiority. Puritanism, to the extent that it focused on self-reliance, hard work, and financial success, proved to be fertile ground for the growth of CAPITALISM.

Because only church members could vote in Massachusetts, church membership was of overriding importance in the community. In order to join a Puritan congregation, one had to be justified—or converted or born again into faith. However, JUSTIFICATION was not sufficient for church membership. To join the Saints, one had to be certified by the minister and the congregation. The prospective church member had to testify to a conversion experience that impressed his or her audience as genuine. SANCTIFICATION followed justification and was the continuing proof that the person was, in fact, a member of the elect.

It is not difficult to see how this process could encourage righteousness and intolerance, not to mention intrusiveness. It was one's duty, as it were, to spy on the behavior of one's neighbor, lest church membership be bestowed on one undeserving. For many modern readers, the treatment of Hester Prynne in Nathaniel Hawthorne's (1804–1864) *The Scarlet Letter* (1850) constitutes the defining portrait of these aspects of the Puritan character. Hester, convicted of bearing an illegitimate child, is forced to wear a scarlet letter "A" (for *adulteress*) emblazoned on her chest for all to see—and thus to be the subject of continuous public scrutiny and censure.

**Hester Prynne**

This nineteenth-century engraving of Hester Prynne and Pearl from *The Scarlet Letter* delivers a strong sense of the social isolation that the pair faces. People are staring, even pointing, at them, and they keep their distance. Hester, used to this treatment, keeps her eyes level and looks straight ahead. Pearl turns to look at the group of children who are, presumably, taunting her.

## A Model of Ecclesiastical Government

It is important to remember that the Puritan settlers envisioned their migration to America as an "errand into the wilderness," in the words of the Reverend Samuel Danforth. They came not only to escape persecution but also to accomplish something never done before in the history of the world: to establish in America a model of government that was both civil and ECCLESIASTICAL.

Unfortunately, many factors combined to shatter the dreams of those first immigrants. During the English Civil Wars (1642–1651), Parliamentarians—who tended also to be Puritans—and Cavaliers (supporters of absolute monarchy)—who tended to be members of the Church of England—battled for control of both church and state. The winners (the Parliamentarians led by Oliver Cromwell) established a government that New Englanders hoped would be built on the principles they had established. However, to win the war and govern in England, Cromwell and his supporters could not afford to be intolerant and exclusionist, and New Englanders watched in horror as Cromwell's government accepted various heretics and heresies into the fold. Thus, American Puritanism began to diverge from English Puritanism, and New England was left to find a purpose for itself other than functioning as a model for English civil and ecclesiastical government.

This questioning of purpose was amplified when it became clear that the children of the first generation of Saints would not all follow their parents. Many children of Saints could not testify to a conversion experience and many became completely taken up with the things of this world—focusing on outward signs of success to the detriment of spirituality. This diminishing sense of purpose led to the frequent preaching of sermons known as JEREMIADS. The term *jeremiad* comes from the name of the prophet Jeremiah and connotes a tale of sorrow or disappointment. Puritan jeremiads followed a specific formula that included references to the courage and faithfulness of the founders of the colony, crying out against current sins among the youth, and calling for a return to earlier virtues.

## American Literature in the Colonies

Sermons, including jeremiads, are one of the three kinds of literature handed down to us by our Puritan forebears—the other two being devotional poetry and history. (Fiction, including drama, was regarded as trivial and corrupting.) Sermons in particular were a crucial part of Puritanism because they were considered the doorway through which most Saints were led to accept grace. Because of their belief in predestination, Puritans did not believe in a cause-and-effect relationship between sermons and conversion; they would reject as preposterous the idea that if a person went to church and listened to sermons, he or she would be saved. Rather, they believed that there were things one might do to prepare the way for irresistible grace, and listening to sermons was chief among them.

A typical sermon had three major parts. The preacher began with a biblical text, which he EXPLICATED. The preacher then explained what laws and lessons might be derived from the text. Finally, he demonstrated how the text and laws applied to everyday life in New England. Puritan sermons and histories were written in plain style, like their churches, unadorned, clear, and straightforward. Similes and metaphors (such as those used by the English poet and priest John Donne (1572–1631) in his sermons) were regarded with suspicion, and clarity and logic were considered of utmost importance. The sermons delivered by Puritan ministers were neither simple nor emotional; instead, they were lengthy, almost legal, disquisitions that required both attention and analysis.

## William Bradford (1590–1667)

In many ways, William Bradford's *Of Plymouth Plantation* (1630–1650) is as much a jeremiad as it is a history. Beautifully written, it attempts to understand God's purpose in the founding of the colony and why the colony did not fulfill its original purpose. Thus, Bradford's history, like the jeremiads, becomes a call to the current generation to reclaim the greatness of the earlier times.

In true Puritan fashion, Bradford looks for God's plan even in the wickedness he sees around him, speculating that "the Devil may carry a greater spite against the churches of Christ and the gospel here."

## Cotton Mather (1663–1728)

Among the great writers of history in Puritan New England was Cotton Mather, son of two prominent religious families. Mather's literary output was prodigious, amounting to more than 450 books and articles over his long life. His greatest work, *Magnalia Christi Americana* (1702), is an exhaustive chronicle of the New England settlement written as a series of biographies of its saints.

Mather, an uncommonly well-educated man who spoke seven languages and was the first American-born member of the British

### THE MAYFLOWER COMPACT

Although second and subsequent generations of Puritans wondered what had happened to their dreams of a model society, we can see from the perspective of history that many aspects of American democratic government come directly from the experiences of the first settlers. These were people who insisted on their right to govern themselves, who insisted on limited government, and who insisted on a contractual relationship between the governed and those who lead. The Mayflower Compact, probably authored by Bradford, spells out in the very simplest terms everything necessary for a social contract. The U.S. Constitution is, in many ways, simply a detailed version of the little compact signed on November 11, 1620, by the men of the *Mayflower*. Its essence lies in the willingness of the signatories to be bound as individuals by laws designed for the good of all. Thus, the signers agree to "combine" themselves

> *into a civil Body Politick, for our better Ordering and Preservation, and Furtherance of the Ends aforesaid; And by Virtue hereof do enact, constitute, and frame, such just and equal Laws, Ordinances, Acts, Constitutions, and Offices, from time to time, as shall be thought most meet and convenient for the general Good of the Colony; unto which we promise all due Submission and Obedience.*

While the Puritan settlers in America thought they were establishing a model for theocratic government, they were, without knowing it, paving the way for a democratic model.

Royal Academy of Science, however, also believed in witchcraft and wrote two works about the Salem witchcraft trials: *Memorable Providences* (1689) and *The Wonders of the Invisible World* (1693). During the trials, Mather wrote letters to judges and preached from his pulpit at the Old North Church in Boston declaring his belief that the devil himself was behind the possessions. Mather hoped that the crisis in Salem would actually help motivate people to return to a more active religious life. Although others apologized for their part in the trials, Mather never did, and his reputation with posterity has been damaged by his involvement in the entire episode.

## Covenants and Heresies

In addition to sin and worldliness, Massachusetts Bay Colony was also plagued by religious dissent, perhaps most famously in

### Inoculating Against Smallpox

**Although Cotton Mather was a conservative Puritan minister, he was sufficiently affected by Enlightenment thinking to be interested in science and scientific advancement. Mather, in fact, introduced inoculation against smallpox to America. He first learned of the practice in a letter written by Emanuel Timonious, a doctor in Constantinople, who describes how Africans had inoculated against smallpox for centuries. Mather questioned one of his slaves, Onesiums, who described how he himself had been inoculated. During an epidemic in New England, Mather convinced Dr. Zabdiel Boylston to try the procedure on his son and two slaves.**

**The people of Boston were terrified by the idea of inoculation. Their fear was amplified by the warnings of other doctors. One, a Dr. Douglas, wrote "inoculation is 'an encroachment on the prerogatives of Jehovah, whose right it is to wound and smite.'" Boylston's life was threatened, and Mather's home was firebombed; the perpetrator left a note saying, "Cotton Mather, you dog, damn you! I'll inoculate you with this; with a pox to you."**

**Many of Boston's Puritan clergy, however, supported the concept of inoculation. Others followed, and the idea caught on, at least among some citizens. Within a year or two of the first inoculations, statistics clearly supported the procedure. Only 6 of the 244 people who had been inoculated died of smallpox, whereas 844 of 5,980 who were not inoculated died.**

the case of Anne Marbury Hutchinson (1591–1643). Hutchinson had been a follower of the great Puritan preacher, John Cotton (1584–1652), in England. She and her husband William migrated to Massachusetts in 1634, a year after Cotton did so. In Boston, Hutchinson continued with a practice she had initiated in England: Every Sunday she met, mostly with female churchgoers, after services to discuss the sermon and to express her religious views. The essence of what she taught can be summed up in her own words: "He who has God's grace in his heart cannot go astray." Although that statement in itself may not sound radical, Hutchinson was tried and convicted of heresy in 1637—not only because of *what* she preached but also because as a woman she dared to usurp what was then considered the male prerogative of preaching.

Hutchinson's heresy was labeled ANTINOMIANISM, and she was reacting to what she believed was a betrayal of the true faith on the

**THE TRIAL OF ANNE HUTCHINSON**

**When she was brought to trial for heresy, Anne Hutchinson stood alone before the governor of the colony, John Winthrop; the deputy governor; five assistants; and five deputies. She was accused of maintaining "a meeting and an assembly in [her] house that hath been condemned by the general assembly as a thing not tolerable nor comely in the sight of God nor fitting for [her] sex." Hutchinson more than held her own during her examination, verbally sparring with her inquisitors and inviting them to specify exactly what she had done wrong. She defended her meetings by saying "I conceive there lies a clear rule in Titus that the elder women should instruct the younger." Hutchinson refers to Paul's letter to Titus in the New Testament, in which Paul says, "The aged women likewise, that they be in behavior as becometh holiness, not false accusers, not given to much wine, teachers of good things; that they may teach the young women to be sober, to love their husbands, to love their children, to be discreet, chaste, keepers at home, good, obedient to their own husbands, that the word of God be not blasphemed."**

**Hutchinson very nearly bested the court, but when she declared that she knew she spoke the truth because the Holy Spirit had spoken to her, she condemned herself because Puritans believed that divine revelation stopped with the Book of Revelation; that is, that God no longer spoke directly to people.**

**Thus, Hutchinson was banished from the colony—largely for being a well-educated, charismatic woman with a mind of her own.**

part of many ministers in New England at the time. To understand Hutchinson's heresy, it is important to understand the Puritan concept of the COVENANT. Orthodox Calvinism tended to emphasize the arbitrary nature of God's will, in order to emphasize the complete dependence of humans on His grace.

To some, this concept of the arbitrary nature of God, allied with the idea of predestination, was frightening. These people believed they could never really know if they were among the saved, no matter how hard they tried to examine their consciences and lead good lives. To help believers through this crisis of faith, Puritan leaders began to articulate a "FEDERAL" theology. These ideas of promises or treaties were not new but they began to be emphasized in a new

**The Trial of Anne Hutchinson**

This depiction of the trial of Anne Hutchinson for heresy on November 7, 1637, ennobles Anne by elevating her above the heads of those sitting in judgment on her. Hutchinson's left hand is raised, as if to heaven. Her right hand seems to be bestowing a blessing on the crowd of ministers and magistrates. She was small and delicate, but the power of her faith gave her the strength to defend herself skillfully. "You have power over my body but the Lord Jesus hath power over my body and soul. . . ."

way between 1600 and 1660. Puritan theologians taught that God had originally made a promise to Adam and Eve. God, who can do whatever He wants and does not have to make any promises to anyone, nevertheless chose to bind Himself in a relationship of equality with the first man and the first woman. This first covenant Puritans called the COVENANT OF WORKS. God promised Adam and Eve eternal life in return for certain works or behavior on their part. However, when Adam and Eve failed to keep their end of the bargain—by eating the forbidden fruit—God declared the covenant of works forever and irredeemably broken. Then, beginning with Abraham, God declared a COVENANT OF GRACE, which suggested that anyone who truly tries to believe in God (and the Puritans equated that effort with churchgoing and listening with an open heart to sermons) would be saved. The covenant of grace became a somewhat delicate theological issue for the Puritans because it seemed to contradict the idea of predestination and to suggest that people could actually earn salvation through their behavior—which sounds a lot like the covenant of works. Puritan theologians walked this fine line by arguing that, although each individual, in fact, had the freedom to choose or reject grace, this freedom of will does not negate predestination because God knew from all eternity who would choose salvation and who would reject it. These same theologians also argued that preparing oneself to receive grace by going to church and exhibiting moral behavior was not the same thing as believing that doing good deeds would earn salvation, thereby avoiding the charge of ARMINIANISM.

However, all of this was simply too legalistic for Goodwife Hutchinson, who believed that the ministers were in fact preaching a covenant of works when they reminded people to attend services and read scripture. She believed that the experience of irresistible grace was unmistakable and that once united with Christ in faith, a believer was, in scholar Perry Miller's words, "exempted from all considerations of conduct." This idea, of course, frightened both ministers and government officials because they began to imagine a colony populated by saints who felt no obligation to obey any rules at all—and who really had no need of churches or clergy either.

As this case amply illustrates, the model community established by the Puritans was not a democracy but a theocracy. Although Puritans wanted freedom to practice their own religion, they felt no obligation to extend this privilege to others and dealt quickly and harshly with anyone who dissented from the orthodox Puritan viewpoint.

## Symbols, Symbols, Everywhere

Puritans also believed in the concept of Divine Providence—the idea that God's plan for the universe was by definition good. Thus, no matter what happened to an individual or a community, it was the duty of a saint to find the good in it. This tendency can easily be seen in the work of America's first poet, Anne Dudley Bradstreet (1612–1672), especially in her poem "Some Verses upon the Burning of Our House" (1666). This work in particular exemplifies the tendency to interpret disaster as Divine Providence, while showing the difficulty of maintaining sincere piety in the face of catastrophe. Bradstreet knows that the possessions lost in the fire that consumed her home are God's to give and take away. Nevertheless, she recalls those possessions lovingly:

> **Here stood that trunk, and there that chest,**
> **There lay that store I counted best.**

It is this concrete detail and the very human sorrow at such a loss that appeal to modern readers. What appealed to Puritan readers, however, is the fact that Bradstreet manages to overcome her regret and place her personal disaster in the context of Divine Providence:

> **Then straight I 'gin my heart to chide,**
> . . . . . . . . .
> **Thou hast a house on high erect,**
> **Framed by that mighty Architect,**
> **With glory richly furnished**
> **Stands permanent though this be fled.**

Puritans also believed that God's plan for the universe could be discerned in His creation; that is, through the observation of nature, one could come to understand God and His plan. When later romantic writers and transcendentalist philosophers, such as Ralph Waldo Emerson, began to advocate PANTHEISM, they were not far from their Puritan roots, although they did not recognize the link. Perry Miller notes that Puritan ministers "verge[d] so close to pantheism that it . . . [took] all their ingenuity to restrain themselves from identifying God with Creation." Although Puritans certainly were not Pantheists, both Puritans and Pantheists have the same tendency to see the universe and all its creatures as SYMBOLIC. It is, perhaps, no surprise that many of the great works of American literature have at their hearts symbols that suggest a larger, METAPHYSICAL reality. From Hawthorne's scarlet letter to Melville's great white whale, to Huck Finn's river, to Frank Norris's octopus, American writers have repeatedly written profoundly symbolic works that give their tales, whether superficially realistic or not, metaphysical dimensions.

Puritans also tended to engage in a kind of biblical interpretation called TYPOLOGY. Through typology, Puritan theologians and ministers would analyze a "type"—a person, event, or concept from the Old Testament—as a foreshadowing of the New Testament "antitype," or the fulfillment of the promise of the type. For example, one could interpret the story of Jonah's three days in the belly of a whale as a type of Christ's three days in the grave. Thus, the story of Jonah prefigures Christ's resurrection. This kind of interpretive strategy was later expanded to include using Old Testament events to forecast or explain current events, as when Puritan ministers interpreted their journeys to America as parallel to—or a type of—the exodus of the Israelites from Egypt.

The poet Edward Taylor (1642–1729), a Puritan minister whose work was not discovered until the twentieth century, is a master in the use of typology, which he employs in the creation of some of the most beautiful religious poetry ever written. In "He Sent a Man Before Them," for example, Taylor writes:

**Is Josephs glorious shine a Type of thee?**
**How bright art thou? He Envi'de was as well.**
**And so was thou. He's stript, and pick't, poore hee,**
**Into the pit. And so was thou. They shell**
**Thee of thy Kirnell. He by Judah's sold**
**For twenty Bits, thirty for thee he'd told.**

For many, Taylor's poetry has become a potent symbol of the true piety of the earliest settlers. Over the years, popular misconceptions have led to many negative stereotypes about the Puritans, not the least of which is that they were hypocrites—people more concerned with their neighbor's piety than their own—people who pretended to have religious faith in order to be socially acceptable. Though there were certainly hypocrites among the colonists, most of the original settlers were individuals of true piety. Taylor also shatters the stereotype of Puritans as prudish otherworldly types who wanted nothing to do with the pleasures of this world. Though his object is always religious, his poetry is rich with the imagery

### ARTHUR MILLER'S *THE CRUCIBLE*

In 1953, Arthur Miller's (1915–2005) play *The Crucible* opened on Broadway. The play was a fictionalized account of the Salem witchcraft trials of 1692. Miller was interested in the witchcraft trials partially because he believed that events taking place in the United States in the 1950s had an uncanny resemblance to those that transpired in Salem centuries earlier.

The events that concerned Miller were the investigations conducted by Wisconsin Senator Joseph McCarthy. The political climate of the era included a strong element of anti-Communism, which McCarthy exploited. He began by accusing 57 State Department employees of being Communist spies. Soon, anyone who held relatively liberal opinions became subject to accusation and investigation. The manner in which McCarthy conducted his inquiries created mass hysteria throughout the nation because he encouraged people to believe that Communists would soon overrun America. Many intellectuals and liberals had, in fact, joined the Communist Party in the 1930s, in reaction to the Great Depression and the profound economic inequality they perceived. Many of these people had left the party during the war years and after, disillusioned by the Communist government in the Soviet Union. When McCarthy questioned such individuals, he took the position that the only way they could convince him of the sincerity of their current beliefs was to point the finger at their prior associates, "outing" friends and colleagues who still held Communist beliefs.

Miller saw in this situation strong parallels to the Salem trials. In both cases, it seemed as though the accusers could get away with attacking anyone, without ever having their own behavior or motives questioned. In both situations, the accused were condemned by the simple act of accusation; they were assumed to be guilty. In both situations, anyone who questioned the sanity of the process would soon find him or herself among the accused. Miller's play seems to ask the question: "Is there something in the American character that leads to such witch hunts?"

and emotion—even the sensuality—of love. Although the object of Taylor's love is God, the language and emotion are profoundly human.

Typology, too, has become a part of the American character. Americans have, it seems, always regarded themselves much as their Puritan forbears did, as a people with a special mission ordained by God. The concept of MANIFEST DESTINY, a phrase coined in 1845 by John L. O'Sullivan, for example, was used to justify and ennoble America's westward expansion. Like the Puritans—who saw themselves not merely as settlers in a new land but as chosen people destined to prepare the way for Christ's second coming—Americans saw their westward move not as land-grabbing or as a response to an exploding population but as part of God's larger plan for the universe.

## Witchcraft

When many Americans think of the Puritans of New England, they automatically think of the witchcraft trials that were held in Salem, Massachusetts, in 1692. This is an unfortunate association because the trials—although they undoubtedly capture the imagination—are not particularly representative of Puritanism, Puritan thought, or Puritan behavior.

Every schoolchild knows the basic outline of the events that transpired in Salem, Massachusetts, beginning in the winter of 1691 and ending in September of 1692. A group of village girls and a West Indian slave named Tituba began to accuse neighbors of the practice of witchcraft. Before the hysteria ended, 185 people were accused; 59 people were brought to trial; and 20 people were executed. Some modern scholars have noted that the vast majority of those executed were women over the age of 40, many of whom were widows with a fair amount of property, and they attribute the scare to both greed and MISOGYNY. Others note that the 1680s were a time of rapid change and many crises—such as floods, disease, Indian attacks, and fires—and attribute the hysteria to a kind of collective posttraumatic stress syndrome. Still others cite economic causes, noting conflicts between the rising MERCANTILE class and farmers and landowners. Others point out that the accusations allowed common people to threaten those in power.

Whatever the cause of the hysteria, the Salem witchcraft trials and their aftermath became a turning point in the history of New England. People increasingly questioned the old religious values and began to accept a more secular view of life. The hopes that engendered the great "errand into the wilderness" were dashed, but out of the crucible came a new kind of society in which Puritan values and ideas persisted but were modified by ideas from the European Enlightenment and other sources.

# 3. Aspects of Colonial American Culture

Although American literature and culture were deeply influenced by Puritanism in the seventeenth century, a very different set of ideas played a significant role in shaping American culture throughout the eighteenth century. These ideas had their roots in Renaissance HUMANISM.

In the seventeenth century, scientists and philosophers began to question religious authority and to see human reason as the ultimate tool in the discovery of truth. The movement that resulted from this shift in attitude was called the ENLIGHTENMENT. Enlightenment philosophers encouraged people to doubt and question what they had been taught, to think for themselves, and to use reason and observation in analyzing the world around them. This philosophy was particularly popular among members of the new merchant class, both in Europe and in the American colonies, who themselves began to question the rights of kings to rule. The middle class began to wonder why they should continue to support such an institution. Enlightenment philosophers also believed in the separation of church and state, in the idea of basic human equality, and in the idea that the universe was governed by natural law. Enlightenment philosophers were not atheists, but their faith, known as deism, was based on what has been called a "clockmaker" deity. That is, they believed in a god who created the universe and all the laws of nature—but once that creation was accomplished, this god withdrew from involvement and allowed the mechanism to work on its own—like a watchmaker winding up a clock. Thus, Enlightenment philosophers denied the possibility of miracles and believed that truth was to be found through scientific study of the laws of nature. They believed that human beings were born in a state of innocence and were corrupted by a corrupt society. The concept of "natural man," articulated by Jean-Jacques Rousseau (1712–1778), suggested that "all men were created equal" and that all humans possessed as their birthright the freedom to choose, a natural compassion, and the urge to perfect themselves and their surroundings.

These ideas will sound familiar to every modern American because they became the heart and soul of the American Revolution and shaped the Declaration of Independence and the Constitution. However, although these ideas were very powerful in shaping

American democracy, they did not prevent the growth of the institution of slavery in America.

## The Growth of Slavery

Although New England developed a large merchant class and populous cities, the southern colonies moved in a quite different direction. From the beginning, colonies such as Virginia and the Carolinas were settled with profit in mind, with early settlers hoping to find precious metals and gemstones for the taking in the new land. Although these dreams were not fulfilled, settlers discovered a different kind of wealth in the vast stretches of virgin soil. In Virginia, tobacco flourished, whereas in the Carolinas and Georgia, rice grew well in the swampy coastal lands. These crops, although profitable, were labor intensive. Originally, large landowners were able to rely on the work of INDENTURED SERVANTS. Typically young men, indentured servants would agree to work for a landowner for a period of years—usually six or seven—in return for the price of passage to the New World. When their period of indenture was complete, the freed servant would be given "freedom dues," usually a plot of land, seed to plant, and perhaps a gun.

The first African people to arrive in America landed in Jamestown, Virginia, in 1619 aboard a Dutch ship; the ship's owners sold them as indentured servants to settlers in exchange for food and other supplies. For many years, in fact, Africans working in the fields in the American South worked side-by-side with English servants and were given their freedom at the end of their period of indenture just as the English servants were. Intermarriage between whites and blacks, while not common, did occur. Over the next generation, events in England began to reduce the number of indentured servants who made the ocean crossing to come to America. The plague that ravaged England in 1665 killed many who might otherwise have sought their fortune in the colonies. The London fire of 1666 resulted in the need to rebuild the city, which in turn resulted in more jobs for young laborers there. In America, restrictions on available land in some colonies led to unrest among newly freed indentured servants. These factors began to effect a change in attitude of landowners toward their African servants, and by the late seventeenth century the system of enslaving Africans for life that had been employed in the Caribbean for many years, began to be used in America. Massachusetts was the first colony to legalize slavery—in 1641—and Georgia the last—in 1750.

Slavery, in all its degradation and brutality, did not arise at once in America; gradually, over the years, attitudes evolved and

### Slave Laws

**The laws regarding slavery throughout the thirteen original colonies evolved over the years; each law was designed to empower the slave owner or limit the slave. In 1639, for example, a Virgina statute prohibited slaves from bearing firearms. Various laws were enacted regarding MISCEGENATION. In the beginning, these laws mandated whippings as punishment; later they included fines and banishment from the colony for the white person involved in the "crime." Despite these laws, white masters often impregnated black slave women, which led to laws regarding the status of the children. Eventually, it was decided that all the children born to an enslaved woman, regardless of who the father was, would be condemned to slavery.**

**Laws were enacted to define precisely what kind of "property" slaves were. Some laws said they were CHATTEL. Later laws defined slaves as "real estate" that could be used—as could land and homes—as collateral for debts. Some of the most brutal laws were enacted to punish those who attempted to escape from slavery. Indentured servants, like slaves, often tried to run away; typically their punishment was time added to their period of indenture. Because slaves served for life, increasingly brutal penalties were enacted. Cutting off ears and branding runaways were typical, legally sanctioned punishments. Laws were even enacted that limited slave owners' abilities to free their slaves.**

laws and statues were enacted that gave slave owners greater and greater control over slaves. In order to justify the control, which was economic in origin, people began to claim that Africans were subhuman and that white skin was superior to black. Even members of the clergy began to cite biblical texts to justify enslaving Africans. Laws were enacted to prohibit intermarriage and to provide for increasingly brutal punishments for running away or stealing on the part of slaves. Thus, the institution evolved.

Most Africans were brought to the New World from the West Coast of Africa. There, African merchants would sell as slaves people they had captured in the interior who had been forced to walk as many as 1,000 miles to the coast. Loaded onto ships, the captives would then endure the nearly three-month trip to America. The sheer brutality of the conditions aboard ships staggers the imagination. Captives were chained together in a sitting or prone position, so tightly packed as to make movement impossible. They lay in their own excrement, sometimes chained to dead companions for days.

Diseases such as yellow fever, smallpox, and dysentery spread rapidly through the ships and sick people were often simply tossed overboard. Altogether it is estimated that between one and two million people died during the crossings from Africa to the Americas.

## The Life of Olaudah Equiano

Some of what we now know of the experience aboard slave ships comes from the personal narratives (sometimes referred to as SLAVE NARRATIVES) of persons who experienced the crossing. Among the most famous of these stories is *The Interesting Narrative of the Life of Olaudah Equiano or Gustavus Vassa, The African* (1789), the first autobiography written by a freed slave living in England. Equiano (c. 1745–1797), as he explains in this autobiography, was born in Essaka, an Igbo village in the kingdom of Benin in West Africa. The son of a king, Equiano was captured when he was eleven years old and sold into slavery. The boy was familiar with slavery because his father owned slaves. However, it is important to note that slavery in Africa at the time was quite different from the slavery Equiano would find in the Americas. In Africa, skin color was not the issue that it was later in America, and slaves were often freed and adopted into the families of their former owners.

Equiano's story tells of his capture in Africa, his transportation to Barbados, then to Virginia, where he was sold to Michael Pascal, an officer in the British Navy. Equiano's master sent the young man to school in England and took him along on his shipboard travels all over the world. In 1766, at the age of 21, Equiano bought his freedom. He continued his career as a sailor, often working aboard ships as a steward or hairdresser. He even took part in an expedition to find a passage to India across the North Pole, commanded by John Phipps. On his return to England, Equiano converted to Christianity and became active in the movement to abolish slavery. His book was a financial as well as popular success, and when Equiano died, he left an estate of £950 (about $160,000 today).

Equiano's description of the conditions aboard a slave ship are vivid and disturbing, and perhaps consciously crafted to resemble the idea of hell itself:

> **The closeness of the place and the heat of the climate, added to the number in the ship, which was so crowded that each had scarcely room to turn himself, almost suffocated us. This produced copious perspirations, so that the air soon became unfit for respiration from a variety of loathsome smells, and brought**

> on a sickness among the slaves, of which many died, thus falling victims to the improvident avarice, as I may call it, of their purchasers. This wretched situation was again aggravated by the galling of the chains, now become insupportable and the filth of the necessary tubs [buckets used as toilet facilities], into which the children often fell and were almost suffocated. The shrieks of the women and the groans of the dying rendered the whole a scene of horror almost inconceivable.

Equiano's narrative became an important document in the fight to abolish slavery and was particularly powerful at the time because many Europeans and colonists believed that Africans were subhuman and incapable of being educated. Equiano, with his eloquence and his grasp of Enlightenment philosophy with its emphasis on "natural rights"—the rights that are owed to every human being just by virtue of being human—made many question these stereotypes. Equiano proved beyond a shadow of a doubt that Africans were capable of rationality, learning, and religious piety.

## Slavery in the Northern Colonies

Although most people associate slavery with the American South, it is important to remember that there were slaves in all thirteen colonies until after the American Revolution, when many northern states finally

### Was Olaudah Equiano Born in Africa?

Led by scholar Vincent Carretta, some historians have begun to express doubts about Equiano's claim that he was born in Africa, kidnapped, and sold into slavery in America. There is in existence a baptismal record indicating that Equiano was actually born in South Carolina and documents from his time in the Royal Navy say the same. Because Equiano never used the name Olaudah Equiano before he wrote his book (he was always known as Gustavus Vassa, the name given him by his master), some scholars believe he made up the name as part of his effort to claim he was born in Africa. Much of what Equiano says about his childhood in Africa could have been taken from other accounts, such as Anthony Benezet's *Some Historical Account of Guinea* (1772). Scholars who believe Equiano is telling the truth about his origins point out the fact that it would not be unusual for a slave to have inaccurate records, nor would it be unusual for Equiano to have mixed up the dates of his transportation to the Caribbean because he was so young when he undertook the journey. A third group of scholars maintains that it does not really matter whether Equiano was born in Africa. He was crafting a work that was intended to galvanize its readers against slavery and was true to the experience of all of those who had been captured and enslaved.

### THE SELLING OF JOSEPH

Samuel Sewall is a figure who seems to stand as a monument to changing times in New England as the seventeenth century ended and the eighteenth began. A devout Puritan and one of the judges at the Salem witch trials, Sewall is remembered today for his diary, which is a tremendous resource for understanding the Puritan way of life and the changes that were threatening it at the time, and for one of the earliest tracts written against slavery, *The Selling of Joseph* (1700). This tract is divided into three parts. The first part uses scriptural sources to argue that whites and blacks are all God's children, and, as such, have "an equal right unto liberty." The second part suggests that indentured servitude is much superior to slavery not only morally but also practically because servants who have their freedom to look forward to will work harder than slaves. In the third part, Sewall denies that the Bible approves of slavery and argues that "these Ethiopians, as black as they are, seeing they are the sons and daughters of the first Adam, the brethren and sisters of the last Adam, the offspring of God; they ought to be treated with a respect agreeable." Sewall adds that a man who holds slaves "forfeit[s] a great part of his own claim to humanity."

Although *The Selling of Joseph* is remarkable as the first antislavery work in New England, modern readers would find many of Sewall's attitudes offensive because he did not believe in integration and did not want importation of more blacks to America.

abolished the practice. Many of the founders of the United States, including John Hancock, George Washington, and Benjamin Franklin, owned slaves. The fact that slavery in the North never grew to the proportions that it did in the South has everything to do with economics and little to do with morality. In general, slaves were better treated in the North, but abuses occurred there as they did in the South.

## Phillis Wheatley (1753–1784)

Phillis Wheatley was among the slaves who lived in the North, although her story is anything but typical. She was born in Africa in 1753 or 1754 and brought to New England in 1761. There, she was purchased by John Wheatley, a Boston merchant, as a personal maid for his wife, Susanna. Susanna Wheatley, who quickly recognized that Phillis was a remarkably intelligent child,

**Phillis Wheatley**

This portrait of Phillis Wheatley appeared in the introductory material to her collection of poems, published in London in 1773. Wheatley sits in the standard pose of the thoughtful writer, a quill in her right hand, her left hand at her chin. She is dressed in the fashion of the middle-class woman of the time.

though frail and sickly, began to teach her to read and write. The child learned English quickly, then progressed to Latin. By the time she was a teenager, she was better educated than most men in colonial America. She became a celebrity in Boston in 1770, when "An Elegaic Poem, on the Death of That Celebrated Divine, and Eminent Servant of Jesus Christ, the Reverend and Learned George Whitefield" was published as a BROADSIDE, and then widely reprinted in newspapers throughout the colonies. Whitefield was an evangelical preacher and is considered, along with John Wesley, a founder of Methodism. He was active in the religious revival known as the Great Awakening. When, in 1773, a collection of her poetry was published, as *Poems on Various Subjects, Religious and Moral,* Wheatley became the first African American and the first slave to have a published book of poetry. Because of the prevailing notion among many Americans that Africans were inferior to whites and incapable of being educated—much less of writing poetry—the prefatory material to the volume included the testimony of Wheatley's master that she had, in fact, written the poems herself, as well as a letter to that effect signed by a number of prominent Bostonians.

Wheatley's poetry is quite conventional in subject matter and style. Many of her poems were ELEGIES, including one about George Washington. Her style was neoclassical, in the manner of Dryden and Alexander Pope. She tends to write in rhymed, HEROIC COUPLETS, to use classical forms such as elegies and epyllions, or short epics, and to include allusions to classical mythology, in which she was well schooled. At the time she wrote, such luminaries as Benjamin Franklin praised her work, while Thomas Jefferson (1743–1826) remained unimpressed. Today, critics speculate on the constraints under which Wheatley labored. Was her work so conventional because of her situation? Had she been raised as a free woman, would her poetry have been more inspired and original? However one chooses to answer those questions, Wheatley's accomplishments remain remarkable.

In only one of her poems does she mention race explicitly, and her tone is gracious and subtle, in keeping with her style:

**On Being Brought from Africa to America**

**'Twas mercy brought me from my Pagan land,**
**Taught my benighted soul to understand**
**That there's a God, that there's a Savior too:**
**Once I redemption neither sought nor knew,**
**Some view our sable race with scornful eye,**

> **"Their colour is a diabolic dye."**
> **Remember, Christians, Negroes, black as Cain,**
> **May be refin'd, and join th' angelic train.**

In this poem, Wheatley accepts a view held by some at the time that Christianity was the real issue separating white from black. What made Africans "barbaric," in the words of those who attested to the genuineness of her work, is that they were not Christian. Before the institutionalization of slavery in America, the English and English colonists tended to accept the view that enslavement was for non-Christians only and they wanted to free those slaves who converted. Thus, Wheatley is affirming the Enlightenment idea of basic equality in suggesting that, once the African is Christianized, the African will be on a level with whites.

In "To the Right Honourable William, Earl of Dartmouth," Wheatley also refers to her status as a slave. She suggests that perhaps her devotion to the idea of freedom stems in part from her personal history:

> **Should you, my lord, while you peruse my song,**
> **Wonder from whence my love of Freedom sprung,**
> **Whence flow these wishes for the common good,**
> **By feeling hearts alone best understood,**
> **I, young in life, by seeming cruel fate**
> **Was snatch'd from Afric's fancy'd happy seat;**
> . . . . . . . . . .
> **Such, such my case. And can I then but pray**
> **Others may never feel tyrannic sway?**

Dartmouth had recently been appointed principal Secretary of State for North America, and Wheatley's poem paints him as someone who will champion the cause of the colonies against the tyranny of the monarch:

> **No more, America, in mournful strain**
> **Of wrongs, and grievance unredress'd complain,**
> **No longer shalt thou dread the iron chain,**
> **Which wanton Tyranny with lawless hand**
> **Had made, and with it meant t'enslave the land.**

Wheatley's choice of words in this paragraph of verse is quite telling; the colonies are enslaved much the same as she is. However, as with many slaves in America around the time of the Revolution, Wheatley seems to present some hope that the rhetoric of liberty will apply to them.

## The Economics of Colonization

The economic theory that was prevalent in the world during the colonial period in America was known as MERCANTILISM, a term coined by the Scottish economist Adam Smith (1723–1790). Mercantilism was, in Smith's formulation, the opposite of a free-market system, which he advocated. At the time Smith began to write, most nations believed that the only form of real wealth was gold or silver, and all nations competed for what they believed was a limited amount of wealth. The wealthiest nation was the one that was self-sufficient, so as not to have to trade its gold and silver to buy goods from other nations.

Thus, nations developed controls—such as TARIFFS—to try to ensure a favorable balance of trade—that is, to ensure that they sold more goods to other nations than they had to buy from them. This economic theory resulted in frequent warfare because countries believed there was only so much wealth to be had, and they often sought to obtain it by taking it from their enemies. It was the mercantile theory of economics, in fact, that led to the colonization of America. If a country such as England could have colonies from which it imported raw materials and to which it could sell finished goods at a profit, it could ensure a favorable balance of trade.

Thus, England enacted laws to ensure its own economic stability with little regard for the interests of its colonists. For example, Navigation Acts passed by Parliament in the 1650s and 1660s prevented foreign-owned ships from trading with the colonies, forced colonists to trade certain goods only with England, and required that the colonists ship all other imports through England. Clearly, such laws were disadvantageous to American merchants; because they were essentially forced to sell to the British, they could not get the best prices for their goods. At first, this was a minor issue, but as the colonies grew and the merchant class became larger and more powerful, these laws and others like them, including the infamous Tea Act of 1773, which led to the Boston Tea Party, became more and more problematic—and, some historians contend, were a major cause of the Revolution.

Adam Smith, who was read by many of the most prominent people in the colonies, opposed mercantilism and advocated a free market. He said that the wealth of a nation was not entirely

**Adam Smith**
This etching was crafted in 1790 by artist John Kay, who was known as a miniaturist and a caricaturist. Smith is portrayed holding a walking stick and pointing at a book, perhaps his own *The Wealth of Nations* (1776), which laid the foundation for American politics and economics. Smith is hatted and bewigged in the style of the day.

dependent on how much gold it had but on all of the goods and services it could produce. He said that governments should not interfere in economics because, if people were simply left to pursue their own self-interest, they would produce enough goods to serve the needs of the entire population. This is called LAISSEZ-FAIRE economics. Smith said that free markets were guided by an "invisible hand." What he meant by this is that if a product is scarce, people will be willing to pay more for it. The rise in price creates an incentive for someone to make the product, thus ending the shortage. As more manufacturers compete to make the product, the price goes down. This is now known as the "law of supply and demand." Many of those who wanted to declare America independent from England were motivated by the idea of free trade and a free marketplace, which would be financially advantageous to American merchants.

## The Great Awakening

The popularity of Smith's economic ideas is an index of the growing secularization of New England society as the century progressed. In physics, it is said, for every action there is an equal and opposite reaction. As the colonies became more secular and religiously diverse and as the philosophies of the Enlightenment began to bring science to the fore and move religion into the background, a major reaction—an evangelical religious movement called the Great Awakening—occurred, beginning in the 1720s and becoming most powerful in the 1740s. This movement, which called for a return to religious piety, began in the middle colonies of Pennsylvania and New Jersey. Revivalist preachers taught that true religion came from the emotions—the heart—not from reason—the head—and they encouraged people to rely again on the revealed word of the Bible rather than on mere reason.

One of those who carried the revivalist feeling throughout the thirteen colonies was the Reverend George Whitefield (1714–1770), for whom Phillis Wheatley had written an elegy. Whitefield, an English Methodist, traveled through the colonies; his sermons drew such large audiences that he was often obliged to preach outdoors. His ideas were not fundamentally different from what the Puritans had taught—that humankind was sinful and completely dependent on God for salvation. What was different was how the sermons were delivered. Whitefield wept, shouted, gestured, and threatened, creating an absorbing performance that was as interesting as any stage play. Converts often reacted in a similar manner to the preaching—by fainting, convulsing, and weeping. Whitefield's preaching had the

### ▪ ▪ ▪ ▪ Sinners in the Hands of an Angry God ▪ ▪ ▪ ▪

"Sinners in the Hands of an Angry God" is the title of a sermon preached by Johathan Edwards in Enfield, Connecticut, on July 8, 1741. The audience's response to the sermon was passionate; it is said that Edwards was unable to complete it because of the cries of the congregation. It is one of the most famous sermons ever delivered in America and is the work for which Edwards is perhaps best remembered today.

Edwards chooses for his text "Their foot shall slide in due time" (Deut. 32:35). He tells his listeners that the text should serve to remind them that they are always on the verge of destruction and that is only by the grace of God that they are not at every moment damned. Edwards then repeats his point using a simile that has become famous:

> *The God that holds you over the pit of hell, much as one holds a spider, or some loathsome insect over the fire, abhors you, and is dreadfully provoked: his wrath towards you burns like fire; he looks upon you as worthy of nothing else, but to be cast into the fire . . . You have offended him infinitely more than ever a stubborn rebel did his prince; and yet it is nothing but his hand that holds you from falling into the fire every moment. It is to be ascribed to nothing else, that you did not go to hell the last night; that you was suffered to awake again in this world, after you closed your eyes to sleep. And there is no other reason to be given, why you have not dropped into hell since you arose in the morning, but that God's hand has held you up. There is no other reason to be given why you have not gone to hell, since you have sat here in the house of God, provoking his pure eyes by your sinful wicked manner of attending his solemn worship. Yea, there is nothing else that is to be given as a reason why you do not this very moment drop down into hell.*

effect of making his hearers believe that everyone was equal before God, and his simple message appealed to simple people: Believe and you will be saved.

Puritans in New England (now referred to as Congregationalists) split between the evangelical "New Lights" and the conservative "Old Lights." The Reverend Charles Chauncy (1705–1787) did battle for the conservatives, while Jonathan Edwards (1703–1758) was the great spokesman for the New Lights. Edwards, a graduate of Yale College, read widely in the texts of the Enlightenment and was particularly interested in the psychological ideas of John Locke

(1632–1704). In his youth he believed predestination was "a horrible doctrine," but after a conversion experience he began to see the idea as "exceedingly pleasant, bright, and sweet," and he became an ardent defender of fundamental Puritan theology. He preached predestination—the idea that salvation was an arbitrary choice on the part of God that no human works could influence—and held to the basic Calvinist idea of irresistible grace—the idea that conversion came from God and could not then be lost through one's behavior.

In 1729, Edwards inherited his grandfather's ministry at a church in Northhampton, Massachusetts. In 1733, the spirit of revival came to Northhampton, and within six months, 300 new members were admitted to Edwards's church. This phenomenon interested Edwards, and he conducted a careful study of the conversion experiences of those who had joined the church. He published this psychological/religious study in 1741 as *The Distinguishing Marks of a Work of the Spirit of God.* Edwards held that the "bodily effects" of conversion—by which he meant the emotional behavior of converts, which included speaking in tongues, swooning, convulsions, and so on—were not truly distinguishing marks of conversion; however, he did say that when the divine spirit visits a person, the body is often affected. Both Edwards and his wife, the former Sarah Pierrepont, reported having mystical religious experiences. After meeting George Whitefield, Edwards's style of preaching changed, leading to a tremendous revival of spirit in his church, about which Edwards wrote in *A Faithful Narrative of the Surprising Work of God* (1738). Although Edwards's delivery was never as dramatic as Whitefields's, his rhetoric was powerful. He is today recognized as one of the greatest preachers ever, and his sermons are still read as masterful efforts to rouse emotions and bring listeners to religion.

The great scholar of Puritanism, Perry Miller, has described Edwards as the first true American philosopher. He studied psychology and wrote on how language could be used to evoke emotions; he argued that beauty was as important to ethics as it was to art; and he regarded the natural world as a source of revelation from God, a position that would later be taken up by Ralph Waldo Emerson and the Transcendentalists. His works about human emotions—the affections—influenced later philosophers, including William James.

# 4. The Literature of the American Enlightenment

Benjamin Franklin's *Autobiography* (1791) tells an amazing tale, one that has attained the status of myth. Every American knows the essence of the story: From humble beginnings, Franklin rose to international prominence through sheer hard work and integrity. Franklin's story is often cited as the very model of the "American dream," and there is a strong sense that it could have happened nowhere but in America. While the British essentially ignored their colonies for many years until they needed new tax revenues in the 1760s, Americans developed their own culture, which did not include the ideas of inherited nobility and strict social hierarchies. Franklin's origins would have sharply limited his ability to rise in status had he been born in England, for example. Yet another reason Franklin's story is so quintessentially American is that his life and thinking unite two dominant streams in American thought: Puritan ideas of morality and Enlightenment philosophy.

## Franklin's Puritan Roots

Franklin's parents were members of Boston's Old South Church, and Josiah Franklin taught his children what is now known as the "Protestant work ethic," the importance of hard work and integrity in all one's business dealings. Later, his son Ben would embody this philosophy in one of his famous sayings, "Early to bed and early to rise, makes a man healthy, wealthy, and wise."

Franklin was conscious of his father's teaching throughout his life, and he earned his initial reputation as a printer by dint of plain hard work. In his *Autobiography,* he recalls that while printing a history of Quakerism he would often continue working until after midnight.

Franklin was also influenced by his early study of Puritan texts. Among the books Franklin read was Cotton Mather's *Bonifacius* (Essays to Do Good) (1710), which, Franklin says, "perhaps gave me a turn of thinking that had an influence on some of the principal future events of my life," a typically modest statement from a man whose civic contributions were legendary.

Like his Puritan forebears, Franklin accepted without question the idea that personal wealth, or the accumulation of private property, was the reward of a virtuous life, an idea that some believe is the foundation of American capitalism, which, in turn, has had a tremendous impact on the formation of the American character.

### The Wit and Wisdom of Benjamin Franklin

Most people know that Benjamin Franklin authored *Poor Richard's Almanac* and are aware that this work was peppered with proverbs and sayings. However, many people might be surprised at how many familiar sayings were originally created by Benjamin Franklin. Just a few of the most famous include: "Early to bed and early to rise, makes a man healthy, wealthy, and wise"; "Haste makes waste"; "A penny saved is a penny earned"; and "Never leave that till tomorrow which you can do today." Clearly, all of these admonitions show the influence of Franklin's Puritan background.

One saying that demonstrates some of his urbane wit and is not so well-known—but perhaps should be—is "Fish and visitors smell in three days"—a handy phrase to have when dealing with relatives who overstay their welcome. Franklin was such an effective diplomat partly because of his quick and sophisticated wit. He seemed to have a response at hand for nearly any situation. After his wife's death, Franklin proposed marriage to a French widow, who turned him down because of her devotion to her late husband. To try to change her mind, Franklin claimed to have visited heaven in a dream. There, he said, he saw the widow's husband married to his wife. "Come, let us revenge ourselves," he said.

Franklin also wrote a number of very pointed satiric essays in the period before the Revolution that used wit and irony to satirize actions of the British crown. In one such essay Franklin presents "Rules by Which a Great Empire May Be Reduced to a Small One." One rule that he articulates, for example, is this:

> *However peaceably your Colonies have submitted to your Government, shown their affection to your interest, and patiently borne their grievances, you are to* suppose *them always inclined to revolt and treat them accordingly. Quarter troops among them, who by their insolence may* provoke *the rising of mobs, and by their bullets and bayonets* suppress *them. By this means, like the husband who uses his wife ill from* suspicion, *you may in time convert your* suspicions *into* reality.

## Franklin and the Enlightenment

As much as Puritanism influenced Franklin, he was much more deeply influenced by the ideas of the Enlightenment, or the Age of Reason. For example, Franklin's attitude toward wealth—which many might label a typically American attitude—was also influenced by Enlightenment ideas about property. The philosopher Thomas Hobbes (1588–1679) had argued that property rights existed only within nation-states and that, therefore, the monarchy's property rights were paramount. However, John Locke (1632–1704)—who, along with Jean Jacques Rousseau (1712–1778), profoundly influenced American Enlightenment thought—disagreed. He believed that human beings had a natural right to anything with which they had mixed their labor, that such rights existed before nations were constituted, and that nations were created to protect property. The importance of property to Locke can be seen in his list of natural human rights: life, liberty, and property. Like Locke, Franklin was a materialist—but he always leavened his materialism with the instinct for civic good.

Despite the influence of his family's Puritanism, Franklin's religious beliefs were not Puritan but Deistic, in keeping with most of those who held enlightened views. Deism is fundamentally a rejection of religious authority—the tenets and dogmas of traditional religion—and is based on the power of human reason to discover the truth about religion. Deists believed in religious tolerance, in the idea that each individual should have the freedom to believe as conscience dictated. Because of this, Deists are sometimes known as freethinkers. It is probably fair to say that Franklin's beliefs are representative of many of the founders of America; they are certainly reflected in both the Declaration of Independence and the Constitution.

Deists, influenced by the new science and the thinking of such theorists as Isaac Newton (1642–1727), rejected the idea that God interfered in the working of nature. They believed that God created the universe and the laws of nature and then abandoned creation to those laws. That is, Deists do not believe in miracles; they believe that even the most mysterious phenomena are capable of being understood through reason and the scientific method. They also believe that the same laws operate throughout the universe. In a sense, all science since Newton has been based on these ideas about the relation of God to the universe.

Another aspect of Franklin's character as a man of the Enlightenment was his notion of moral perfectibility. Thus, Franklin embarks on a plan to develop thirteen virtues, one at a time. He reveals later in the *Autobiography* that a friend of his wondered why Franklin had not included humility as one of the virtues. Franklin adds humility to his list but notes, with characteristic wit, "I cannot boast of much success in acquiring the reality of this virtue, but I had a good deal with regard to the appearance of it."

Yet another sense in which Franklin embodied the ideal of the American Enlightenment was his interest in science. Franklin is perhaps most famous for his experiments with electricity. Most people know that Franklin experimented with lightning, using a key tied to the string of a kite. He conducted this experiment in 1752 in order to determine whether lightning was an electrical current, and proving, in fact, that it was. This discovery came at a time when many uneducated people believed that lightning was a punishment from God rather than a natural phenomenon. On a more practical level, he invented the lightning rod, which saved many homes from destruction by lightning; typically, he refused to patent the invention, believing that he should not charge money for ideas that helped humanity.

Franklin's electrical experiments were published internationally, and he became well known in scientific circles. He was made a member of the British Royal Society in 1756 and was granted a number of honorary doctoral degrees for his work on electricity. He invented many of the terms still used today in discussing electricity, including *battery, conductor, condenser, charge, discharge, electric shock,* and *electrician.*

Franklin not only helped draft the Declaration of Independence (1776) but also his diplomatic work in France during the American Revolution was a crucial factor in ensuring victory for the colonists. He lived to see the beginnings of the new nation, including the inauguration of George Washington (1732–1799) as the first president. He died, at the age of 84, on April 17, 1790.

## An American Farmer

It is a mistake to assume that Franklin's *Autobiography* is simply that: the story of one man's life. Franklin writes very self-consciously—that is, he is very much aware of certain literary CONVENTIONS. He is aware that in telling his own story, he is also creating an American myth; he is aware of how his audience is likely to react, and he consciously selects those events from his life that contribute to the myth of the man of humble beginnings who rose to prominence through the use of reason in a country where hierarchies of nobility no longer existed.

The same can be said for Hector St. John de Crèvecoeur's *Letters from an American Farmer* (1782) In this work, too, the author is much less interested in telling his life story than he is in defining a character he calls the American Farmer, and he sets forth this character as the model of the ideal human being of the Enlightenment, free from corrupt society.

**Franklin's Experiment**

In this painting, Benjamin Franklin performs his famous experiment with a kite, in which he demonstrated, for the first time, that lightning is electricity. Franklin never wrote an account of this experiment, but the chemist Joseph Priestly did. His source was Franklin himself:

> . . . He took the opportunity of the first approaching thunderstorm to take a walk in the fields . . . The kite being raised, a considerable time elapsed before there was any appearance of its being electrified . . . [but] . . . just as he was beginning to despair of his contrivance, he observed some loose threads of the hempen string to stand erect. . . . Struck with this promising appearance, he immediately presented his knuckle to the key, and (let the reader judge of the exquisite pleasure he must have felt at that moment) the discovery was complete. He perceived a very evident electric spark.

The boy helping with the experiment is Franklin's son, William, who was actually 21 at the time.

### Franklin's Inventions

Franklin, as a man of the Enlightenment, was always interested in science, and, as most people know, experimented with electricity and even invented the lightning rod. He invented other practical objects as well, many of which we still use today.

For example, Franklin invented bifocals. Because he got tired of switching glasses in order to be able to read, he cut the lenses on two pairs of glasses in half, then united a half lens from each pair in a single frame, solving the problem with one ingenious stroke.

He invented the Franklin stove. Most of Franklin's neighbors heated their homes with wood-burning fireplaces, which were the cause of many house fires. Franklin not only founded the first volunteer fire department to deal with this problem but he also invented a metal stove that provided more heat than an open fireplace and was safer.

Having sailed across the Atlantic Ocean many times aboard ships, Franklin was well aware of the dangers involved in such travel. He suggested that ships be built with watertight compartments, following a Chinese model, so that if one part of the ship sprung a leak, it could still stay afloat.

Franklin himself said, "Of all my inventions, the glass armonica has given me the greatest satisfaction." Franklin created this musical instrument after hearing Georg Handel's *Water Music* (1717) played on glasses tuned by being filled with various amounts of water. Franklin's instrument included glasses that were nested inside one another, did not require water, and could be played with a foot pedal.

Born Michel-Guillaume-Jean de Crèvecoeur (1735–1813) in Normandy, France, Crèvecoeur changed his name when he became a citizen of New York in 1765. Although French by birth, Crèvecoeur was an ANGLOPHILE. After many years working as a surveyor, he married and settled in on a farm in central Pennsylvania. *Letters from an American Farmer,* as the title explains, is constructed as a series of letters from "James," as Crèvecoeur refers to himself, to Mr. F.B., an Englishman. It is the first book ever to attempt to answer the question, "What, then, is the American?" If that question sounds a bit strange today, it is important to remember that

### D. H. Lawrence on Classic American Literature

In a funny and insightful collection of essays, British writer D. H. Lawrence (1885–1930) romps through American literature, looking at some of its most distinguished writers and classical works. Because American readers share a cultural background with the writers, they are sometimes surprised by Lawrence's skepticism—but his *Studies in Classic American Literature* (1923) highlights how different American literature is from other national literatures.

One of Lawrence's essays looks at Benjamin Franklin's *Autobiography*. It begins, "The Perfectibility of Man! Ah heavens, what a dreary theme!" referring to the list of moral virtues Franklin hoped to develop. Lawrence highlights the utter simplemindedness of such an attempt. "I am many men. Which of them are you going to perfect? I am not a mechanical contrivance." Lawrence goes on to elaborate, debunking the idea that living in America could erase the evil that has always mingled with the good in humankind. "The ideal self!" he fairly shouts. "The perfectibility of man, dear God! When every man as long as he remains alive is in himself a multitude of conflicting men."

Lawrence also has something to say about Crèvecoeur's *Letters from an American Farmer*. He notes that

> *Franklin is the real* practical *prototype of the American. Crèvecoeur is the emotional. . . . NATURE. I wish I could write it larger than that, NATURE. Benjamin overlooked NATURE. But the French Crèvecoeur spotted it long before Thoreau and Emerson worked it up. Absolutely the safest thing to get your emotional reactions over is NATURE.*

However, says Lawrence, Crèvecoeur was "an emotional liar," adding that he tried to put "Nature-Sweet-and-Pure in his pocket. But nature wasn't having any, she poked her head out and baa-ed."

Lawrence points out that Crèvecoeur has to leave out a great deal of truth in order to maintain his fiction about the goodness of nature. This is why, eventually, "he trotted back to France in high-heeled shoes, and imagined America in Paris." Just as Lawrence sees Franklin as ignoring the beast inside humans, he believes Crèvecoeur ignores the beast that is at the heart of nature, lurking out there in the forest.

until this point it was not universally thought that Americans were a distinct group, different from their European counterparts. It is this point that Crèvecoeur attempts to make in his definition.

Crèvecoeur's American is an independent farmer, a person who owns his own land, feeds his family from what he grows, and lives with little interference from government or laws. Like Crèvecoeur, the American farmer is not educated; Crèvecoeur says his father gave him "no other education than the art of reading and writing." Crèvecoeur and his farmer may even be called anti-intellectual, in that they were opposed to abstractions and "book learning." Quite the contrary, the farmer is educated through his (for Crèvecoeur does not conceive that a woman alone might be a farmer, though he acknowledges that many farm wives work just as hard as their husbands) intimacy with nature.

## The Romantic in Nature

Crèvecoeur's farmer is a romantic; he finds both truth and beauty in nature and derives his own nobility from nature itself. Crèvecoeur's romanticism is clearly revealed in his descriptions of nature, as when he listens to "the sweet love tales of our robins, told from tree to tree." However, nature for Crèvecoeur does not seem to include the wilderness. He notes that those who move to the edge of the wilderness and live by hunting become barbaric—like the wilderness itself—and can only be rehabilitated by taming the land—by cutting down the forests and farming, and by creating a garden out of the wilderness. This effort is what civilizes them and makes them true Americans.

Some modern feminist critics have seen in Crèvecoeur's language about the "taming" of the wilderness a sexual metaphor that unmasks the romantic Crèvecoeur as an imperialist conqueror who "rapes" the land. The extent to which taming nature is crucial to Crèvecoeur's ideal of the American is illustrated in his tale of a nest of hornets. This "curious republic" of insects lives in his house and by "kindness and hospitality" have become "quite harmless; they live on the flies, which are very troublesome to us throughout the summer; they are constantly busy in catching them, even on the eyelids of my children." In America even hornets are peaceful and industrious and, like the land, can be made to conform to human reason.

According to *Letters from an American Farmer,* the tremendous bounty of nature in America is part of the very soul of the farmer. He must labor, but his labor is amply rewarded by the land itself.

The European, says Crèvecoeur, becomes an American "by being received in the broad lap of our great *Alma Mater,*" the great mother—the American landscape. In Europe there is no real motivation for ordinary people to do their best, whereas in America "labor is founded on the basis of nature, *self-interest.*" A farmer who is working for himself and his family will put forth his best effort: "Men are like plants; the goodness and flavor of the fruit proceeds from the peculiar soil and exposition in which they grow. We are nothing but what we derive from the air we breathe, the climate we inhabit, the government we obey, the system of religion we profess, and the nature of our employment. Here you will find but few crimes; these have acquired as yet no root among us."

## Freedom of the American Farmer

Freedom is another important characteristic of the American farmer. The farmer possesses "freedom of action, freedom of thoughts." And the land itself, the owning of property, is the foundation of that freedom. The form of government that grew in America, where everyone is noble and hierarchy and rank do not exist, allows each individual to become what nature intended. "We have no princes, for whom we toil, starve, and bleed: we are the most perfect society now existing in the world. Here man is free; as he ought to be." Crèvecoeur's American Farmer is nearly a perfect example of Jean-Jacques Rousseau's "natural man"—the innocent creature each human was meant to be.

The ideal of the American Farmer became one of the guiding myths of American democracy and a recurrent theme in American literature. R. W. B. Lewis (1917–2002) in *The American Adam* (1955) might almost be quoting from Crèvecoeur when he describes the American literary hero—whom he dubs the "American Adam"—as "an individual emancipated from history, happily bereft of ancestry, untouched and undefiled by the usual inheritances of family and race; an individual standing alone, self-reliant and self-propelling, ready to confront whatever awaited him with the aid of his own unique and inherent resources." Those writers whose works portrayed such heroes—writers such as Emerson, Whitman, and Thoreau—Lewis calls "the party of hope." However, many writers believed that this ideal American never really existed at all and that corruption comes from within the human soul, not from social structures. These writers Lewis calls the "party of irony." Writers such as Hawthorne, Melville, and James often begin their works with characters very similar to Crèvecoeur's farmer—innocent, self-reliant, hopeful—and then trace their downfall as they find the worm in the soul of humanity, as they confront evil, decadence, and human frailty.

## The Final Letter

Crèvecoeur himself seems to follow a downward path. His final letter, Letter XII, is written in a paroxysm of fear and sorrow. His farm is in the path of the American Revolution, and he lives in terror lest he and his family be destroyed. As a TORY he is caught in a war whose rationale he neither understands nor accepts—and he feels his life is in danger. His attitude toward the Revolution, in fact, is made quite clear in the Preface to the first edition of the *Letters* in which he describes himself as an "eye-witness" to "transactions that have deformed the face of America." In Letter XII, Crèvecoeur decides to take his family westward and to live among a tribe of Native Americans—a plan that Rousseau would have undoubtedly approved. However, instead he returns to France to look into his children's inheritance. Leaving his family in 1778, Crèvecoeur headed East and was captured by the British and held as a spy until 1780, when he was allowed to leave the country. He published *Letters* in London and then traveled to France. He returned to America in 1783, as French consul to New York. By that time, his wife was dead, his farm burned, and his children living in Boston. Crèvecoeur died in France in 1813.

## Thomas Jefferson (1743–1826)

Thomas Jefferson was, if possible, even more multitalented than Benjamin Franklin. He was an architect, an artist, a poet, a musician, a politician, a diplomat, a farmer, and a scientist, among other things. One measure of the extent of his talent is a quip made by President John Kennedy at a glittering White House dinner for Nobel Prize winners. Kennedy described the evening as "the most extraordinary collection of talent, of human knowledge, that has ever been gathered together at the White House—with the possible exception of when Thomas Jefferson dined alone." Jefferson was truly a person of the Enlightenment, a person who valued human reason beyond all other abilities, who was infinitely interested in the world around him, and who devoted his life to acquiring as much knowledge as possible.

Jefferson was born into a well-to-do Virginia family on April 13, 1743 and was educated at the College of William and Mary. In 1770, he began work on a mansion, which he dubbed Monticello

### ▪ ▪ ▪ ▪ MONTICELLO ▪ ▪ ▪ ▪

Jefferson's home at Monticello is a reflection of the man. He once said, "Architecture is my delight, and putting up and pulling down one of my favorite amusements," and he spent many years of his life constructing and reconstructing his home. He loved both the art and the science of architecture; his home struck the eye with its symmetry and beauty. His original design was inspired by ancient Roman design and by the Renaissance architect Andrea Palladio (1508–1580); after his stay in France, Jefferson incorporated French elements, including a dome with a central, circular skylight called an oculus, and beds that were set back in alcoves. Despite these European influences, however, Monticello has been described as uniquely American in its fusion of the various architectural elements.

Jefferson was as much an inventor—a man of science—as was Franklin, and he included many innovations in the design of his home. Two dumbwaiters carried wine from the basement to the dining room, and Jefferson's office boasted a copying machine of his own devising, a contraption that linked two pens in such a way that when he wrote, an exact copy of his text was made. Skylights and large windows ensured that most of Monticello's 43 rooms were flooded with natural light. Five indoor toilets, though not flushable, were improvements over the outdoor variety.

In 1987, Monticello was added to the World Heritage List, a U.N. program that aims to preserve international treasures. In 1993, on the 250th anniversary of his birth, the American Institute of Architects awarded Jefferson a Gold Medal for "a lifetime of distinguished achievement and significant contributions to architecture and the human environment."

("little mountain" in Italian). Jefferson designed the home and spent many years completing it.

## Jefferson's Writings

In 1774, Jefferson wrote a political pamphlet, entitled "A Summary View of the Rights of British America" in which he enumerated "the united complaints of his majesty's subjects in America," adding that "The God who gave us life gave us liberty at the same time: the hand of force may destroy, but cannot disjoin them." Jefferson is alluding here to John Locke's concept of natural rights, the rights he believed every person possesses by virtue of being human.

These sentiments clearly foreshadow the language of the Declaration of Independence.

During the Revolution, Jefferson served in the Virginia Assembly, where he created a number of laws limiting the rights of large-plantation owners, which Jefferson labeled the "pseudo-aristocracy." One such law abolished ENTAIL. In 1779, Jefferson introduced into the Virginia legislature a bill to allow freedom of religion, an important piece of legislation because at the time no state, indeed no nation, had such a law. The bill read, in part, "all men shall be free to profess, and by argument to maintain, their opinions on matters of religion." Many Virginians opposed the bill because they regarded it as an assault on Christianity itself. When legislation was finally enacted in 1786, thanks to the continuing efforts of James Madison, Jefferson—who was the American Minister to France at the time—wrote, "It is honorable for us to have produced the first legislature who had the courage to declare that the reason of man may be trusted with the formation of his own opinions." A true man of the Enlightenment, Jefferson valued human reason above all other faculties.

## Later Years

A slaveholder himself, Jefferson was opposed to slavery, although he did not consider blacks to be equal to whites. As a man of science, he urges the question of the differences between the races to be studied but concludes by saying, "I advance it therefore as a suspicion only, that the blacks, whether originally a distinct race, or made distinct by time and circumstances, are inferior to the whites in the endowments both of body and mind."

Nevertheless, Jefferson advocates an end to slavery because he believes that the manners and morals of Americans are "depraved" by slavery, turning masters into "despots." He notes also that "With the morals of the people, their industry also is destroyed," pointing out that slaveholders become lazy through forcing others to work for them. He worries that slaves may revolt and speculates that God may be on their side if they do. He continues,

> **The spirit of the master is abating, that of the slave rising from the dust, his condition mollifying [improving], the way I hope preparing, under the auspices of heaven, for a total emancipation, and that this is disposed, in the order of events, to be with the consent of the masters, rather than by their extirpation [extermination].**

### JEFFERSON AND SALLY HEMINGS

During Thomas Jefferson's first term as president, there were rumors that he had fathered children with one of his slaves, Sally Hemings. Jefferson would not discuss the subject, and his only known response to the accusation was in a private letter written in 1805, in which he denied the story.

Over the years since, descendants of Hemings have held that Jefferson did father either some or all of Hemings's six children. With the growing sophistication of DNA testing, it became possible to investigate the validity of the Hemings's claims, and in 1998 Dr. Eugene Foster and a group of geneticists conducted a study of descendants of both Sally Hemings and Thomas Jefferson. Because they were checking for Y chromosomes, they only looked at descendants of Hemings's sons; they found that one son, Easton, was related to Thomas Jefferson. The eldest son, Thomas Woodson, was not.

Although this would seem to suggest that Jefferson was Easton's father—and may have been the father of Hemings's four daughters—there are other possibilities. At the time that Easton Hemings was conceived, there were at least 25 male relatives of Jefferson, who would have had the same Y chromosome, living in Virginia—one of whom was Jefferson's younger brother, Randolph. Thus, although Easton is indeed related to Jefferson, he may not be a direct descendant. Nevertheless, the Monticello/Thomas Jefferson Memorial Foundation declared in 2000 that "the best evidence available suggests the strong likelihood that Thomas Jefferson and Sally Hemings had a relationship over time that led to the birth of one, and perhaps all, of the known children of Sally Hemings." The Thomas Jefferson Heritage Society in 2001 insists that Randolph is the more likely candidate as the father of Hemings' children.

Jefferson retired to his home at Monticello in 1809 and spent much of his time in retirement in designing, planning for, and establishing the University of Virginia. He died on July 4, 1826, precisely on the 50th anniversary of the signing of the Declaration of Independence.

# 5. The Literature of the American Revolution

Most historians agree that the American Revolution was inspired by four major eighteenth-century trends: the philosophies of the Enlightenment, the Great Awakening, the expansion of the British Empire and the wars that resulted from British global ambitions and economic disagreements between Britain and the colonies. The Enlightenment furnished the ideas about independence, equality, and self-government that led to revolution. The Great Awakening led to a greater sense of unity among the colonies and to more independent thinking on the part of many people who began to question the wisdom of established religion. As Britain expanded its global reach, it became increasingly dependent on income from the colonies, both through trade and taxation. The French and Indian War taught the colonists both that European military strategies did not work particularly well in battles in America and that the colonists had to rely on one another for protection. These trends, combined with a series of specific events, including the Stamp Act, the Sugar Act, the Navigation Acts, and the Townshend Acts, led many colonists to consider revolution.

## Thomas Paine (1737–1809)

One of those demanding revolution was Thomas Paine, an Englishman who, at the age of 37, immigrated to America. Arriving in Philadelphia in November 1774, he began working as a journalist, writing for the *Pennsylvania Magazine* about a number of social issues, including slavery.

*Common Sense,* a pamphlet published on January 10, 1776, is the writing for which Paine is remembered today. The 47-page broadside sold 120,000 copies in three months, and total sales may have reached as many as 500,000—at a time when the total population of the colonies was only 2.5 million. In *Common Sense,* Paine argues that the colonies should declare independence from British rule and says his arguments are based "on nothing more than simple facts, plain arguments, and common sense." Independence, when Paine was writing, was not a popular idea—which gives some sense of how influential his pamphlet was.

*Common Sense* begins with a discussion on the origins of government, a discussion that, in style and substance, is similar to many such discussions by Enlightenment philosophers.

Government, says Paine, is nothing more than "a mode rendered necessary by the inability of moral virtue to govern the world"; it is a way for groups of people to ensure their own security. Government comes from the will of people as they form societies, says Paine, and though monarchy as a form of government may have risen out of convenience, monarchy on the face of it is an absurd form of government:

> In England a king hath little more to do than to make war and give away places; which in plain terms, is to empoverish the nation and set it together by the ears. A pretty business indeed for a man to be allowed eight hundred thousand sterling a year for, and worshipped into the bargain! Of more worth is one honest man to society, and in the sight of God, than all the crowned ruffians that ever lived.

This passage in particular gives a sense of Paine's superb use of common, everyday language and common-sense reasoning in making his case.

**PAINE'S VIEW OF THE BIBLE**

**Paine's view of the Bible was that it is allegorical, an idea that outraged many of his contemporaries. But, he says,**

> ***the Church of Rome could not erect the person called Jesus into a Savior of the world without making the allegories in the book of Genesis into fact. . . . All at once the allegorical tree of knowledge became, according to the Church, a real tree, the fruit of it real fruit, and the eating of it sinful. . . .***
>
> ***Why then should the tree of knowledge, which is far more romantic in idea than the parables in the New Testament are, be supposed to be a real tree? The answer to this is, because the Church could not make its new-fangled system, which it called Christianity, hold together without it.***

**Reason, says Paine, the highest of human faculties, cannot accept a literal interpretation of the Bible, a position that many Enlightenment philosophers shared and that is accepted by many today.**

## Other Writings by Paine

During the war, Paine began to write the sixteen papers that were eventually collected as *The American Crisis* (1776–1783). These essays were written in order to defend the revolution and to encourage American soldiers to continue fighting. The first essay begins with the famous words, "These are the times that try men's souls. The summer soldier and the sunshine patriot will, in this crisis, shrink from the service of their country; but he that stands it now, deserves the love and thanks of man and woman." *The American*

*Crisis* was read aloud to soldiers on duty and in homes and taverns throughout the colonies. In the second essay Paine coined the term *United States of America.*

After independence, Paine chose to return to England. There, he wrote *The Rights of Man* (1791–1792), in which he expressed antimonarchist views. The British government banned the work, and Paine himself was indicted for treason—but before he could be tried, he escaped to France, where he was imprisoned—this time by the antimonarchist revolutionaries—for opposing the execution of King Louis XVI. During his time in prison, he wrote *The Age of Reason* (1794–1796), in which he discussed and explained his Deist religious views. As part of his discussion of established religion, he compared the Christian Bible to Greek mythology. In 1794, he was freed from prison with the help of James Monroe and returned to America in 1802.

If Paine expected to be greeted as a hero of the American Revolution on his return, he was deeply disappointed. Most Americans now saw him only as the author of a scurrilous attack on the Bible. Thus, Paine died impoverished, in New York City, on June 8, 1809. A contemporary newspaper reacted to the news of his death with this dismissive comment, "He had lived long, did some good and much harm," but that negative evaluation has changed over the years. Harvard historian Bernard Bailyn calls *Common Sense* "the most brilliant pamphlet written during the American Revolution and one of the most brilliant pamphlets ever written in the English language." His writings helped inspire a nation.

## Patrick Henry (1736–1799)

Another of the hotheaded young men reared on Enlightenment philosophy who demanded justice through revolution was Patrick Henry, one of America's great orators. Unlike other famous speakers of the day, Henry did not allude to Greek and Roman authors and lay out logical arguments. Like the evangelical preachers of the Great Awakening, Henry preferred to cite the Bible and appeal to emotion—at the same time that he referred to Enlightenment ideas, such as natural rights and limited government. His most famous speech was delivered to Virginia delegates in May 1775 in response to a request for support from the Continental Congress. It is the final sentence of the speech—"I know not what course others may take; but as for me, give me liberty or give me death"—that is best remembered. According to those who heard the speech, Henry began by speaking softly, urging those who still believed the king would come around to abandon that hope. As he continued, he raised his voice and called on his listeners to reject the idea that Americans were too weak to stand up to the might of the British military, invoking natural law on behalf of a cause he deems holy. His final words were spoken with great force, and the resolution to support the Continental Congress passed.

Patrick Henry was elected governor of Virginia in 1776 and was reelected four more times. He died in 1799 at the age of 63.

## Native Americans and the Revolution

Few people, if asked to detail the content of the Declaration of Independence, would cite these words, which occur as part of a list of the crimes committed against Americans by the "present King of Great Britain."

> **He has excited domestic insurrections amongst us, and has endeavoured [sic] to bring on the inhabitants of our frontiers, the merciless Indian Savages whose known rule of warfare, is an undistinguished destruction of all ages, sexes and conditions.**

The writers of the Declaration in this passage are referring to the Proclamation of 1763 and its aftermath. At the end of the French and Indian Wars (1750–1763), the British had driven the French from lands west of the Allegheny Mountains and east of the Mississippi River, and from the Gulf Coast into Canada. In order to ensure peace, at least temporarily, the British declared this newly acquired land off limits for colonial settlers and appointed British superintendents to oversee the territory, both of which actions angered colonists. As the original thirteen colonies increased in population, there was increasing pressure to open the lands to the west for settlement, and colonial governments disliked this tampering with their rights to govern what they increasingly perceived as their own land. By the time the Declaration was penned, both the British and the colonists were soliciting help from Native Americans. Ethan Allen of Vermont sent this message to the Iroquois in 1775: "I know how to shoot and ambush just like the Indian and want your warriors to join with me and my warriors like brothers and ambush the regulars." And the British urged members of the Six Nations to "feast on a Bostonian and drink his blood." Ultimately, many Native American tribes did fight in the Revolutionary War, some with the British, others on the side of the colonists. When the war ended, however, colonists used the words of the Declaration and the

### Patrick Henry's Opposition to the Constitution

**Many students of U.S. history may not be aware that the great orator and patriot Patrick Henry staunchly opposed the ratification of the Constitution. Henry argued passionately against the document; he was particularly critical that it contained no Bill of Rights because, he felt, without such protections the central government could easily slide into tyranny. He also focused his attention on the first words of the Preamble, "We, the people."**

> ***Have they said, We, the States? Have they made a proposal of a compact between states? If they had, this would be a confederation. It is otherwise most clearly a consolidated government. . . . I need not take much pains to show, that the principles of this system are extremely pernicious, impolitic, and dangerous. Is this a monarchy like England, compact between prince and people, with checks on the former to secure the latter?***

**Eventually, James Madison promised to add a Bill of Rights. With that promise, Henry relented and Virginia ratified the Constitution. Henry and others proposed twelve amendments, ten of which were added to the Constitution in 1789.**

enmity of some tribes to justify taking the lands of people who were now regarded as enemy combatants. They also, however, took the land of tribes such as the Stockbridges and Oneidas, who had supported the colonial cause.

## The Shot Heard 'Round the World

In 1837, Ralph Waldo Emerson (1803–1882) wrote "The Concord Hymn" in celebration of the first battles of the American Revolution, which took place in Lexington and Concord, Massachusetts, in April 1775. Perhaps the two most famous lines from that poem are, "Here once the embattled farmers stood / And fired the shot heard round the world." Emerson, from the vantage of more than 50 years, was able to see with great clarity the huge impact the Revolution had on world history. For the first time, a colonial people had declared itself independent from its colonizing nation, and a new nation had been founded on the principles of the Enlightenment, principles that included freedom, justice, private property, equality, and self-determination. Politics would never be the same.

Some modern historians take a somewhat more jaundiced view of the Revolution. For example, historian Alan Taylor in *American*

**Patrick Henry**

This painting depicts Patrick Henry uttering the famous words, "Give me liberty, or give me death!" The speech that ended with those words was delivered in March 1775, at St. John's Church in Richmond, where the Virginia legislature was meeting to attack the Stamp Act. The furor over this restrictive British law helped establish the American tradition of peaceful protest.

*Colonies* (2002) notes that the Americans' "empire of liberty" applied only to white people and required the "systematic dispossession of native peoples and, until the Civil War . . . the perpetuation of black slavery." He adds that the "new American empire" also "provided military assistance to subdue Indians and Hispanics across the continent to the Pacific." Thus, he sees the Revolution as a turning point in which former colonists themselves became colonizers. Certainly, to the extent that one sees America as an imperial power, this interpretation will fit in with such a perception.

## The Iroquois Constitution

Most people know that the ideas that underpin the Constitution of the United States are largely derived from Enlightenment philosophy. However, many people are unaware that there was another major source of inspiration: the constitution of the people of the Six Nations, also known by the French term *Iroquois.* This document, which was originally preserved orally, originated between 1390 and 1450, before any contact between Native Americans and colonists. It outlines the governance of a true PARTICIPATORY DEMOCRACY. While drafting the U.S. Constitution, John Rutledge (1739–1800) of South Carolina suggested using the model of the Iroquois League of Nations. Benjamin Franklin was also aware of the Iroquois form of government, having printed minutes of some of their meetings. While the U.S. Constitution created a REPRESENTATIVE DEMOCRACY, it drew inspiration from the Iroquois Constitution.

The Iroquois Constitution was particularly useful to the framers of the U.S. Constitution in that it provided a model of how to join several independent states into a single confederacy. Under the Iroquois document, individual states attempted to deal with disputes within their own borders, only bringing issues to the national level that could not be solved within the state. The Iroquois constitution also guaranteed freedom of speech and religion and specifically portrayed leaders as the servants of the people.

## Remember the Ladies

Abigail Smith (1744–1818) was born in Weymouth, Massachusetts, the daughter of the Reverend William Smith and Elizabeth Quincy Smith. She married John Adams (1735–1826), who would become the second president of the United States in 1764, beginning a marriage that was by all accounts one of history's great romances and partnerships.

Because of John Adams's dedication to the cause of revolution, he and his wife were separated for long periods of time during

**JOSEPH BRANT**

**Joseph Brant (1742–1807), whose Mohawk name was Thayendanegea (which translates as "he places two bets"), was a Native American who staunchly supported the British cause during the American Revolution.**

**Although the six tribes of the Iroquois (which included the Mohawk) had originally pledged to remain neutral as hostilities worsened between the British and the colonists on the eve of the American Revolution, Brant feared that Native Americans would surely lose their land if the Americans won the impending war. In 1775, he traveled to England to meet King George III, a trip that convinced him to support the British.**

**On his return, Brant convinced the Iroquois to join the British in their battle against the colonists. He and the forces under his command fought against the rebels for more than five years in both New York and Ohio.**

their marriage. Thus, Abigail Adams was left the complicated task of managing the household by herself. She did this so well—with such good judgment and efficiency—that they escaped the financial failure that was the fate of many of the young Republic's early public servants. In fact, he wrote to his wife that he was starting "to be jealous, that our Neighbors will think Affairs more discreetly conducted in my Absence than at any other time." Abigail Adams bore six children, five of whom survived infancy. Although she was very self-conscious about her lack of formal education, which showed in her inconsistent spelling and punctuation, she was a prolific letter writer, and her correspondence with her husband makes fascinating reading.

Abigail Adams had strong opinions, especially about the rights of women. She believed that women, like the American rebels, should not submit to laws that did not consider their best interests. She believed that women should be as well educated as men so that they could fulfill their responsibilities to the best of their abilities. Although she did not question the role of women as mothers and homemakers, she believed strongly that education was essential for the performance of that role. Along with her friend Mercy Otis Warren (1728–1814)—playwright, poet, and historian—Adams argued that because women would be the ones to educate the children of the Republic during their early years, it was in the best interests of America to ensure that the women were well educated.

She wrote to John that "If [the new nation] is to have Heroes, Statesmen, and philosophers, we should have learned women."

While John Adams was serving in the Continental Congress in March 1776, his wife wrote to him:

> In the new code of laws which I suppose it will be necessary for you to make, I desire you would remember the ladies and be more generous and favorable to them than your ancestors. Do not put such unlimited power into the hands of the husbands. Remember, all men would be tyrants if they could. If particular care and attention is not paid to the ladies, we are determined to foment a rebellion, and will not hold ourselves bound by any laws in which we have no voice or representation.

John replies, flirtatiously and wittily:

> As to your extraordinary code of laws, I cannot but laugh. We have been told that our struggle has loosened the bonds of government everywhere; that children and apprentices were disobedient; that schools and colleges were grown turbulent; that Indians slighted their guardians, and negroes grew insolent to their masters. But your letter was the first intimation that another tribe, more numerous and powerful than all the rest, were grown discontented.

But Adams—who is often flirtatious and witty herself—is quite serious this time:

> I cannot say that I think you are very generous to the ladies; for, whilst you are proclaiming peace and good-will to men, emancipating all nations, you insist upon retaining an absolute power over wives. But you must remember that arbitrary power is like most other things which are very hard, very liable to be broken.

Adams was disappointed in her hope that the laws of the new country would ensure equal treatment for women, and it was to be nearly 150 years before women were allowed to vote.

Abigail Adams was what would be called today an "active" first lady during her husband's term as president, so much so that she earned the nickname, "her majesty." The Adamses were the first presidential family to live in the White House, which was unfinished, therefore, cold, drafty, and unpleasant. True to form, Adams made good use of the cavernous space by hanging laundry in the East Room.

### The Place of Women in Iroquois Society

The Iroquois nation not only influenced the development of the U.S. Constitution but they also were influential in helping to shape the thinking of nineteenth-century American women as they began to demand the right to vote and other rights that had been traditionally denied them, for example, the right of married women to own property. In this struggle, early defenders of women's rights were deeply influenced by the example of women of the Iroquois Nation. One of the leaders of the women's movement in the nineteenth century, Lucretia Mott (1793–1880), was familiar with women of the Seneca tribe and based many of her ideas on what she knew of these women.

The creation stories of the tribes that formed the Iroquois Nation were based on the idea of a female creator. The world comes into being through the intervention of a pregnant female who is often called Sky Woman. She also is the source of all the plants that feed the people and from whom they obtain their medicine.

In addition, the story is told that, at the founding of the Iroquois Confederacy, a woman selected the first chief of the Confederacy by placing antlers on his head. Since that time, the story explains, women have always had the power to both choose and unseat chiefs.

Iroquois society is MATRILINEAL; that is, descent is traced through the maternal line. People lived in clans that were based on the relationship among females, and when a woman married, her husband left his clan and joined hers. Women divorced husbands merely by telling them to leave the clan.

In Iroquois society, the roles of men and women were different, for example, the men cleared the fields and the women planted and harvested. But there was no sense among the Iroquois, as there often was in American society at the time, that women's work was in any way inferior.

Abigail Adams did not live to see her son, John Quincy (1767–1848), elected to the presidency, although she did see him appointed James Monroe's secretary of state in 1817. She died of a fever in October 1818.

## Slavery in the New Nation

After the Revolution, the thirteen colonies were united under the Articles of Confederation. By 1787, however, it was clear that the

### ▪ ▪ ▪ ▪ Mercy Otis Warren ▪ ▪ ▪ ▪

A friend of Abigail Adams for many years, Mercy Otis Warren is one of the most important women of the Revolutionary War period. She was a poet, a playwright, a historian, and a passionate partisan on behalf of the principles of liberty that underlay the Revolution.

Like most women of the era, Mercy Otis was not formally educated. But when her oldest brother Joseph decided not to go to college, her father allowed her to join her brother James in his studies, and they were both tutored by the Reverend Jonathan Russell. Otis was not the only rebel in her family; it was James who first uttered the phrase, "No taxation without representation."

In 1754, Otis married James Warren, who served in the Massachusetts House of Representatives. The couple had five children. Warren's first work—which was published anonymously—was a play entitled *The Adulateur* (1772), a satire directed against the Royal Governor of Massachusetts. Two more plays followed, *The Defeat* (1773) and *The Group* (1775). All three plays were written in BLANK VERSE, and all were written to be read, not performed. *The Group* also features the Royal Governor, christened Rapatio by Warren, for his "raping" of the colony. In a prophetic moment, one of the characters worries about the effects of the governor's behavior on the people:

*I fear the brave, the injured multitude,*
*Repeated wrongs, arouse them to resent,*
*And every patriot like old Brutus stands,*
*The shining steel half drawn—its glittering point*
*Scarce hid beneath the scabbard's friendly cell*
*Resolved to die, or see their country free.*

In 1805, when she was 77 years old, Warren published her three-volume *History of the Rise, Progress, and Termination of the American Revolution*. Not only was this a brilliant history that included an insider's view but also it was the first book ever deliberately published by a woman who was considered by herself and others as a professional nonfiction writer.

**Declaration of Independence**
Philadelphia artist Jean Louis Gerome Ferris completed this painting in the early years of the twentieth century. It depicts three of the five members of the committee assigned to draft the Declaration of Independence. Thomas Jefferson is standing by the table, Benjamin Franklin is reading, and John Adams sits between them. Not pictured are Robert Livingston and Roger Sherman. The bright sunlight pouring in the window not only illuminates the room but also seems to symbolize the ideas of the Enlightenment.

national government under the Articles had too little power to be effective, a "shadow without substance," as George Washington said.

Thus, in 1787, a convention was convened to draft a new constitution for what would become the United States of America. Unfortunately, the framers of the Constitution did not "remember the ladies." Nor did they, as some of the delegates to the convention hoped, abolish the institution of slavery. For example, in his notes on the discussion about slavery that occurred on August 22, James Madison (1751–1836) writes that slave trafficking is "unreasonable" and "inconsistent with the principles of the revolution and dishonorable to the American character." Still, several southern states refused to join the new union unless slavery was sanctioned by the Constitution. Because southern states in particular were leery of giving up their rights to a national government, several plans were proposed to effect a compromise between northern and southern states. The BICAMERAL legislature was one such compromise. Whereas the Senate was constructed to give each state equal voting power by giving each two senators, the House of Representatives ensured that the people of each state would be represented, with more populous states having a greater number of representatives. Interestingly, the words *slave* and *slavery* do not appear in the Constitution. The compromises that were made with respect to slavery included allowing the importation of slaves into the United States until 1808 and to allow each slave—referred to as "all other persons" (that is, other than free men)—to be counted as three-fifths of a person for the purposes of electing representatives to the House. Indians were excluded from the count. The Constitution also allowed for persons "held to Service or Labor in one state, under the Laws whereof, escaping into another" to be returned—meaning that fugitive slaves had to be returned to their "owners." Although the Bill of Rights, which was added to the Constitution in 1789, does not address slavery, it does say that no person could "be deprived of life, liberty, or property, without due process of law." Unfortunately, at the time, slaves were considered property—not people—so this clause protected slave owners, not the victims of slavery.

The Constitution framers, however, in omitting the words *slaves* and *slavery* from the Constitution had their eyes on history. Although those who opposed slavery may have lost the battle, they won the war. The words did not appear in the Constitution and the institution was eventually eliminated from the land.

# 6. Literary and Cultural Visions of the New Nation

Even before the revolutionary period, American culture had developed distinctive aspects that were peculiarly its own. Among other things, American culture was shaped by cultural contact and military conflict with the Native American peoples; by the presence of African slaves throughout colonial society; by plants and animals native to America; by the tension between "wilderness" and "settlement" in colonial folkways and folklore; by the absence of a deep feudal past and an established church; and, but not least, by its colonial status itself, wherein traditional English customs would often conflict with local American realities. Thus, on the eve of the Revolutionary War, colonial American society showed traces of a "national culture," even if the colonies themselves fell short of a national political union.

After the Revolutionary War, American writers frequently extolled the virtues of the new nation by claiming that its civic freedoms were squarely in line with the philosophy of natural rights. The United States, so went the argument, was *the* Enlightened nation, the first fully rational society in human history. Consider, for example, Benjamin Franklin's essay "Information to those who would remove to America" (1782). Franklin disavows the "mistaken ideas and expectations" of what is to be found in America. Many Europeans arrived in America with the belief that land, slaves, livestock, and tools were all freely available. "These are all wild imaginations," says Franklin. He counsels that, although America does not offer instant great riches to whomever desires them, a person of moderate talents, who works hard at "some profession, calling, trade, or farm" will certainly prosper.

In Europe, a person is known by social status, for example, as a commoner or a gentleman, as it were, but in America, says Franklin, the only question asked of a stranger is "*What can this person do?*" America is "the land of labor." In America, people are free to develop their potential, "there being no restraints preventing strangers from exercizing any Art they understand, nor any permission necessary." That a person is born a commoner is no indication that he or she cannot become a "respectable citizen." America is a rational construct in accord with the laws of nature because its political culture is based on the premise that the free individual (who seeks to realize him or herself) is the most basic of nature's requirements for the good society.

## New Ideas on Education

In the aftermath of the Revolutionary War, the educational system was viewed as crucial to ensuring the success of the new federal framework of government. Through education, citizens would be made aware of the intricacies of the federalist system, and they would also learn their responsibilities as members of a republic.

An important commentator on the link between republicanism and liberal education was Dr. Benjamin Rush (1745–1813) of Philadelphia. Rush graduated from Princeton when he was only fifteen years old. He studied medicine for a number of years and in 1769 was appointed professor of chemistry in the College of Philadelphia, the first medical school in America. Rush was a member of the Revolutionary Congress, which passed the Declaration of Independence in 1776, and was well known for his medical writings and for his liberal views on slavery and racism. His pamphlets on education were controversial.

In his 1798 essay "On the Mode of Education Proper in a Republic," Rush argued, "The business of education has acquired a new complexion by the independence of our country." He believed that the American education system ought to teach the values of patriotism, sobriety, and industry, along with the liberal arts. According to Rush, students should be taught that they do not belong to themselves but to the national community, and that they should aim to succeed in academics not for themselves alone but for the good of the country. Rush says, "I consider it possible to convert men into republican machines. This must be done, if we expect them to play their part in the great machine of the government of the state." Rush supposed that if the United States was to be a society of laws, the moral character of the citizenry could not be left to chance. Reason demanded that, in order to attain political stability, the government ought to pursue a deliberate policy of training up its citizens into "republican machines."

Thomas Jefferson (1743–1826) agreed with Benjamin Rush that a true republican society was inconceivable in the absence of a republican educational system. In his *Report of the Commissioners for the University of Virginia* (1818), Jefferson noted that the goals of primary education were simply to "instruct the mass of our citizens in their rights, interests and duties, as men and citizens." For Jefferson, education was the decisive factor that distinguished a civilized society from a barbarous one. Jefferson was particularly committed to scientific education: He believed that science had a crucial role to play in developing American industry. Without its own industry, the United States would not be able to achieve economic independence from Europe.

In a famous letter to his nephew, Peter Carr, dated August 10, 1787, Jefferson outlined his ideal scheme of education. He advised Carr to study French and Spanish and recommended an exacting course in moral philosophy because "The moral sense, or conscience, is as much a part of man as his leg or arm." Jefferson was a Deist who rejected most schools of theology. He instructed Carr to

> **shake off all the fears and servile prejudices, under which weak minds are servilely crouched. Fix reason firmly in her seat, and call to her tribunal every fact, every opinion. Question with boldness even the existence of a God; because if there be one, he must more approve of the homage of reason, than that of blindfolded fear.**

Like Thomas Paine who professed in his *Age of Reason* (1794) that the true theology derives from the rational study of nature rather than contemplation of the scriptures, Jefferson is skeptical of established churches because they have been the source of great strife throughout human history. Jefferson tells Carr that he ought to read the Bible, but he should be suspicious of the truthfulness of the Old Testament, which contains descriptions of miracles and the like. As regards the New Testament, Jefferson advises that Carr should ponder deeply "the history of a personage called Jesus." Jefferson says that Carr should not rule out the possibility that instead of being the son of God, "born of a virgin," Jesus might well have been a "man of illegitimate birth, of a benevolent heart, enthusiastic mind, who set out with pretensions to divinity, ended in believing them, and was punished capitally [by the Romans] for sedition."

The essence of Jefferson's advice is that Carr should be bold and clear in his thinking, that the power of reason is great and that God gave us the "oracle" of reason precisely that we might know how to use it to understand ourselves and the world around us. Jefferson's last piece of advice to Carr is that he ought to travel, for travel "makes men wiser." However, Jefferson counsels against becoming too enamored of foreign climes; the true purpose of travel, as Jefferson sees it, is to gather knowledge of the world, which may be "usefully" applied to one's own country.

The writer and lexicographer Noah Webster (1758–1843) also meditated on the importance of travel in the liberal model

### WASHINGTON'S FAREWELL ADDRESS

Just as Thomas Jefferson left a legacy of advice on education to his nephew, George Washington advised his fellow Americans on what he perceived as political dangers to be avoided by the new democracy. In his farewell address to the nation, which was printed in a Philadelphia newspaper, the *American Daily Advertiser*, in September 1796, Washington warned against the formation of political parties, especially those that were geographically based; counseled Americans to avoid "permanent alliances" with foreign governments; and urged Americans to "cherish public credit" by ensuring that the country's financial obligations were paid.

Washington feared that political parties, which he referred to as "combinations and associations," would

> *organize faction, to give it an artificial and extraordinary force; to put, in the place of the delegated will of the nation the will of a party, often a small but artful and enterprising minority of the community." He warned that political parties would be likely "to become potent engines, by which cunning, ambitious, and unprincipled men will be enabled to subvert the power of the people and to usurp for themselves the reins of government, destroying the very engines which have lifted them to unjust dominion.*

Unfortunately, even Washington himself was unable to avoid partisan politics. During his presidency, Washington was increasingly identified with the Federalists, who advocated a strong central government, and opposed to Jefferson's Democratic Republicans, who advocated limits on centralized power.

Washington also warned against permanent alliances with foreign governments, fearing that such entanglements would lead the nation into wars and other conflicts. So well heeded was his advice on this subject that the United States did not sign a treaty of alliance with another country until 1949.

He also advised Americans to be careful not to accumulate public debt, and to quickly pay off whatever debts the nation owed, so as not to leave "to posterity the burden which we ourselves ought to bear." This advice, it seems, has not been heeded.

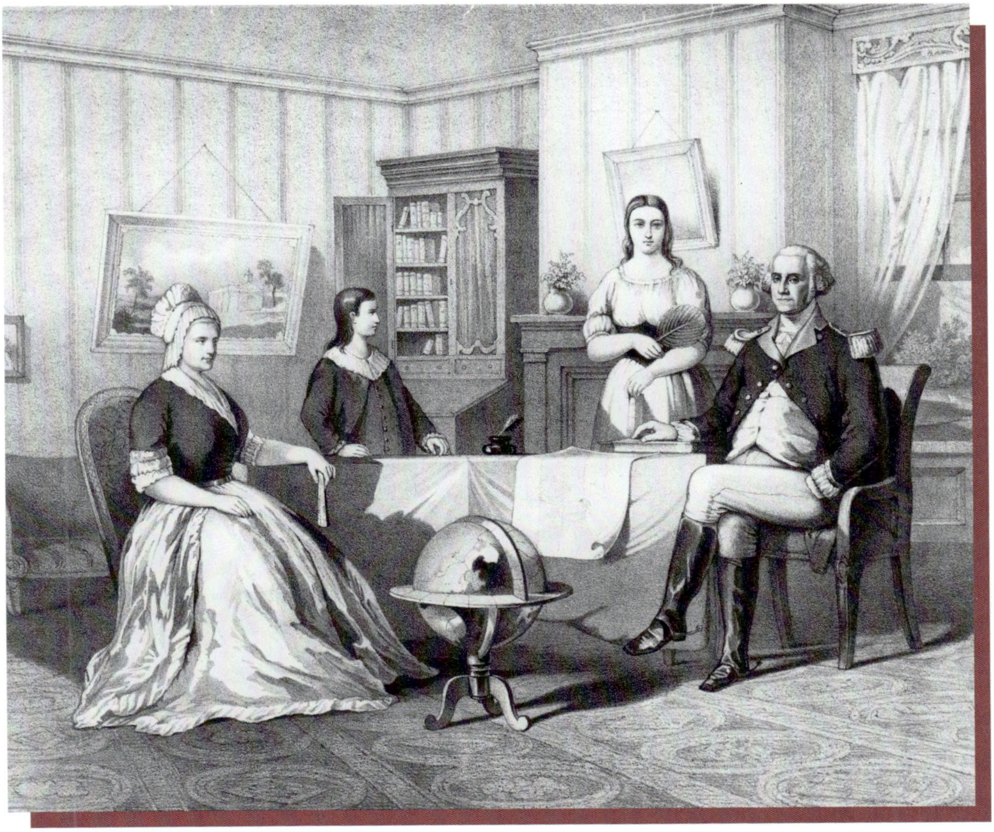

**Washington and Family at the Table**
Painted about 1833, this idealized portrait depicts a noble-looking George Washington, in his military uniform, enjoying a relaxing moment at home with his family. Across from him is his wife, Martha. Two children join them.

of education. In his treatise *On the Education of Youth in America* (1788), Webster argued that "men should travel, and not boys." A boy should be trained up to know and love his own country; he must develop an "attachment" to his own society before he is permitted to reside abroad. Webster believed that too many American youths were educated in Europe, and that this tended to lessen their commitment to their own society. Thus, he said, American leaders ought to build up the American university system so that it would no longer be necessary for Americans to send their sons overseas for a decent education. In a passage that strongly anticipates the arguments of Ralph Waldo Emerson in his famous lecture "The American Scholar," Webster boldly states his position:

> **Americans unshackle your minds, and act like independent beings. You have been children long enough, subject to the control and subservient to the interest of a haughty parent. You have now an interest of your own to augment and defend: you have an empire to raise and support by your exertions, and a national character to establish and extend by your wisdom and virtues.**

It is worth noting that Webster's extensive efforts to establish the uniqueness of American English was based on the assumption that it spoke to the particular conditions of American life. In other words, a national language reflects the cultural, political, geographical, and historical elements that make for a specific "national character." Like Rush and Jefferson, Webster believed that the American national character was only partly realized and that it needed a well-designed educational system to cement its standing throughout the country.

Part of the educational reform movement that swept the new nation was the introduction of the study of *belles-lettres* (literature regarded as art) to college curricula. Literary societies and college theatricals also encouraged an interest in literature, and many an American patriot believed George Berkely's prophesy, in "Verses on the Prospect of Planting Arts and Learning in America" (1751), that the arts would reach their pinnacle in the new land. Colonial literature—which consisted primarily of histories and sermons—would now be replaced by a new national literature.

## New American Fiction

Two of the most popular works of fiction during the early national period were written by women. Susanna Rowson's (1762–1824)

### The Remarkable Susanna Rowson

Although Susanna Rowson's *Charlotte Temple* has spawned fewer feminist interpretations than Hannah Webster Foster's *The Coquette*, Rowson's life itself is a testament to the strength and resourcefulness of women. The daughter of a lieutenant in the Royal Navy, Rowson came to America with her father in 1766. During the American Revolution, Rowson's father's loyalist sympathies led to the family's being held for three years as prisoners of war. All of their property was confiscated, so when the family returned to England after the war, they lived in poverty. Rowson helped to support the family through her writing. She married William Rowson in 1786, and the couple joined a Scottish theater company as actors. In 1793, the Rowsons immigrated to the United States, where they continued to work in the theater. Rowson not only acted in a Philadelphia-based theatrical company but she also wrote songs and plays.

In 1794, Rowson republished as *Charlotte Temple* a novel she had published in England in 1791 as *Charlotte: A Tale of Truth*. *Charlotte Temple* was a runaway best seller in America, going through more than 150 editions. Because she did not own the American copyright to the novel, she made little money from her success.

In 1796, Rowson left the stage to found the Young Ladies' Academy of Boston. Unhappy with the textbooks available to her, Rowson wrote her own. She ensured that the curriculum included mathematics and science, subjects that were seldom taught to women of the era. Rowson ran the school for 25 years; she died in 1824.

*Charlotte Temple* (1791) and Hannah Webster Foster's (1759–1840) *The Coquette: Or The History of Eliza Wharton* (1797) both went through multiple editions and continued to be widely read for more than 50 years. Both works are novels in the sentimental tradition and they treat nearly identical subjects: the seduction of young women by unscrupulous men. Dismissed by critics for many years as unworthy and seldom read or anthologized after the Civil War, *Charlotte Temple* and *The Coquette* have regained a place in the canon of American literature thanks to feminist critics who insisted that the works merited attention. In particular, critics have come to regard *The Coquette* as a critique of the limited opportunities available to women in the new nation. *The Coquette* tells the story of Eliza Wharton, a beautiful, intelligent, and sensitive woman who longs for a life of glamour and excitement and who ignores the advice of family and friends who want her to marry Mr. Boyer, a minister like Eliza's own father. Instead, Eliza flirts with Peter Sanford who eventually seduces her. Ruined and pregnant, Eliza delivers a stillborn child and dies. As is typical of seduction novels of the period, *The Coquette* purports to warn young girls of the dangers inherent in straying from the path of virtue, but the novel can also be read as a protest against a society that forces women into such narrow molds and in which marriage is really the only option available to young women. Eliza can be seen as a rebel against social constraints and the novel as a protest against the lack of freedom for women in the newborn "land of the free."

The novels of Charles Brockden Brown (1771–1910) could not be more different from those of Foster and Rowson. Brown published six novels between 1798 and 1801 (*Edgar Huntly, Arthur Mervyn, Ormond, Memoirs of Carwin the Biloquist, Alcuin,* and *Wieland*) and is often cited as the first American novelist by those critics who discount Rowson and Foster. Brown is said to have "Americanized" the Gothic novel. European Gothic novels, following the pattern established by Ann Radcliffe in *The Mysteries of Udolpho* (1794), usually involved a mystery, an ancestral curse, a brooding villain, and typically took place in ruined medieval castles. Such settings were simply not available in America, so Brown set his works in an American landscape—substituting lonely estates and dark forests for the medieval trappings of the European Gothic. Foreshadowing the works of Edgar Allan Poe (1809–1849), Brown's novels are psychological studies, full of mystery and terror, that seem to challenge the rational ideals of Enlightenment philosophy on which the young country was founded. Humankind is not perhaps inherently good or rational, Brown suggests, and evil lurks even in the halls of democracy.

## New American Poetry

Philip Freneau (1753–1832) became known as "the poet of the American Revolution" because of the poetry he wrote beginning in 1775 satirizing the British and Tory sympathizers. Like many young men of the era, Freneau was inspired to write the great American epic poem. While he was a student at Princeton University, Freneau collaborated with his friend Hugh Henry Brackenridge (1748–1816) to produce a commencement poem entitled "The Rising Glory of

**THE SAD TALE OF ELIZABETH WHITMAN**

**In 1788, the body of an unknown woman was found in a room at the Bell Tavern in Danvers, Connecticut. She had given birth to a stillborn child and had died of puerperal fever. The story was reported on July 29 in the *Salem Mercury* and was widely read throughout the colonies. People were scandalized when it was revealed that the woman was Elizabeth Whitman, the unmarried daughter of a socially prominent Hartford, Connecticut, clergyman. Intelligent and well educated, Whitman was known as an accomplished poet, who had been courted at one time by the poet Joel Barlow. She had been engaged to a cleric who died in 1775 and later broke off her engagement with another clergyman. The child's father and Whitman's seducer is not known, but a future vice president of the United States, Aaron Burr (1756–1836), has been identified by historians as a possible suspect, as has Pierrepont Edwards (1817–1892), the youngest son of the great Puritan divine, Jonathan Edwards.**

**Readers of Hannah Webster Foster's *The Coquette* would have certainly recognized the basic elements of Elizabeth Whitman's story in Foster's fictionalized account. Whitman was a distant relative of Foster's husband, the Reverend John Foster.**

America," which contained a prophecy that America would eventually rule all the land between the Atlantic and Pacific. Influenced by British poets Alexander Pope (1688–1744) and John Dryden (1631–1700), many young men of the era attempted epic poetry with an American cast, including Joel Barlow (1754–1812), who wrote *The Prospect of Peace* (1778), *The Vision of Columbus* (1787), and *The Columbiad* (1807); and Timothy Dwight (1752–1817), who weighed in with *The Conquest of Canaan* (1785). Interestingly, none of these young writers succeeded in writing the great American epic—perhaps because none of them had discovered a truly American form and language. It would be another 50 years before Walt Whitman wrote what is now regarded as the quintessentially American poem—*Leaves of Grass.*

Many critics believe that Freneau did not do his talent justice by writing satirical and topical verse, much of which is forgotten today. But his legacy remains in his great lyrical poems "The Wild

### Freneau's Vision of the American Nation

Philip Freneau's long poem "The Rising Glory of America" (1775) contains many important ideas about the uniqueness of American nationhood. Many nineteenth-century writers explored the cultural, political, and moral implications of these ideas. Freneau opens the poem with an appeal to "the adventurous muse" to help him depict the nobility of the American nation. The poet celebrates America in the Enlightenment fashion, as a natural society whose "laws" are a "pattern" for all the world to follow. He criticizes the example of the Spanish empire in South America for being only concerned with plundering material wealth. The North American continent contains an abundance of uncultivated lands; these lands are destined to become the plantations of thousands of independent farmers. According to Freneau, this fact alone accounts for the manifest superiority of American society over all other nations: for it was widely believed in the eighteenth century that agriculture was the most virtuous of all economic pursuits. Work on the land was intrinsically moral because not only did it produce the necessities of life but it also kept one in touch with the operations of natural law.

"The Rising Glory of America" articulates certain notions of American nationhood that became the typical concerns of American writers throughout the nineteenth century. Freneau portrays America as an *asylum for the oppressed*, a place where men and women are "Secure from tyranny and base controul [sic]." He emphasizes that America is a *frontier culture* and that Americans are an "adventurous" people who delight in "searching out uncultivated tracts" in "our western lands." America is *the first enlightened or universal nation* that properly fits "virtue's plan." Finally, Freneau describes America as a *New Jerusalem* formed by heavenly decree to instruct mankind that the Kingdom of God is at hand. These images of America as nature's nation, as God's nation, and as a nation that contains the future of the world, play an important role in the works of the major writers of the nineteenth century: from James Fenimore Cooper to Ralph Waldo Emerson to Herman Melville and Walt Whitman.

Honey Suckle," "The Indian Burying Ground" and "To a Honey Bee," which foreshadow the romantic nature poetry of William Cullen Bryant (1794–1878). "The Indian Burying Ground" is one of the first works to idealize the character of Native Americans. Inspired by burial customs, Freneau celebrates the vigor of Native

American life. The dead warrior is buried with “His imaged birds, and painted bowl, / And Venison, for a journey dressed.” These accoutrements “Bespeak the nature of the soul, / Activity that knows no rest.”

Like Freneau, Joel Barlow is remembered today not for his satiric and epic verse but for his mock epic poem, *The Hasty Pudding* (1793). Written while he was living in Europe, this charming poem celebrates the simple food and simple life of New England, where

> The invited neighbors to the husking come;
> A Frolic scene, where work, and mirth, and play,
> Unite their charms, to chase the hours away.

Barlow conjures a lovely picture of rural life in New England in the process of praising the cornmeal pudding of his youth.

In the early history of America, the world was changing from one dominated by religious belief to one shaped by scientific knowledge; governments evolved from absolute monarchies to democracies; and men and women began to think of themselves as free people with the right to self-determination. For these reasons, American literature took on the shape it did.

# 7. Women's Voices

When Abigail Adams wrote to her husband, John, who was serving in the Continental Congress of 1776 in Philadelphia, urging him to "remember the ladies," she was enjoining him to ensure that American women had equal rights under the law. She used the language of the American Revolution to remind her husband that tyranny was tyranny, whether exerted by kings and lords or fathers and husbands. Her husband dismissed her with a witty rejoinder, saying the new nation did not count women as full citizens endowed with "inalienable rights." Only *men* were created equal.

Adams' plea to remember the ladies has taken on new meaning in recent years as literary scholars and historians have realized that we tell the story of America's early years as if women had little to do with the construction of a new nation and a new culture. A mere 20 or 30 years ago, only three of the women discussed in this volume would have appeared in any study of American history and literature—Anne Bradstreet, Anne Hutchinson, and Abigail Adams. Others, such as Phillis Wheatley (1753–1784) and Susanna Rowson, would have been considered outside the mainstream of American literature and their writing labeled inferior.

Beginning in the 1970s and 1980s, however, scholars began to realize that they indeed had forgotten the ladies and, in doing so, had largely distorted the truth about the American experience. As Carla Mulford notes in "Writing Women in Early American Studies: On Canons, Feminist Critique, and the Work of Writing Women into History":

> **We had read . . . materials written primarily by an elite group of men whose poetry told of the work of being Christians attempting to thwart the devil while facing personal and community losses. Their prose consisted largely of sermons carrying similar messages or seamless-seeming narratives . . . about so-called savage Indian peoples, disorderly women, uncivilizable Africans, murderous Spaniards, and idolatrous French.**

The material to which Mulford refers is the CANON of early American literature, a set of literary works that experts and historians view as being important in furthering an education and understanding, in this case, of American literature and colonial times. Of course, what an educated person reads is determined also by writers themselves, namely those works from the past which continue to demand attention and response. Obviously, the canon may change over the years as literary tastes change. However, the fundamental list of which writers to read in American literature remained relatively stable for many years and was developed, as Mulford notes, primarily by excluding works that did not seem to fit into the conceptual framework erected by the experts. Almost since the beginning of American literature, most works considered noteworthy by literary experts featured a solitary male protagonist venturing forth into the unknown to find himself. Characters such as Huckleberry Finn, Captain Ahab, Dean Moriarity, Holden Caulfield, Natty Bumpo, and Jay Gatsby come to mind, but the list could go on and on. Women, if they are portrayed at all, appear as little more than plot devices.

## Changes in the Canon

Since the 1970s, however, there have been tremendous changes in the canon of American literature because various groups demanded that their voices be heard and that the threads of their lives be woven into the tapestry that is the American experience. Women were the first to speak up, demanding that scholars take notice of American women writers excluded from the canon simply because they wrote about things that were not deemed part of the heroic tale of American colonialism, not about home and hearth, children, or domesticity. Before long, students were studying neglected women writers, such as Kate Chopin (1851–1904) and Charlotte Perkins Gilman (1860–1935). This attention to women began something of a revolution of attention. Over the next 30 years, the canon was enriched by the works of many others who had been systematically neglected: African American, Hispanic, and Chinese American writers, as well as gay and lesbian writers, Native American writers, and others who had always been part of the American experience but whose works and contributions were marginalized.

### Writing But Not Published

The amount of material available from women during the colonial and revolutionary periods is small. Writing for publication was generally not considered to be appropriate for women during these times. In fact, the story of how Anne Bradstreet's poetry came to be published amply illustrates this belief. It was her brother-in-law who took the manuscript back to England with him without Bradstreet's knowledge and saw to its publication. Bradstreet would probably never have thought to publish her own poetry had he not intervened. How many women wrote but did not publish, and how many others dreamed of writing but did not write at all? In her essay "A Room of One's Own," the British writer and feminist Virginia Woolf wonders what might have happened if Shakespeare had had a sister who shared his literary genius:

> **'Judith' would not have received an education and would have been confined to her parents' home until she was given over to a husband. Her life would have been drudgery from morning to night, and there would have been little time to write. If her genius was great enough, Judith's frustration at not being able to express it might have driven her mad.**

## Diary Literature

Because writing for publication was difficult, very little published poetry or prose written by women exists from the early days of the American experience. There are, however, although not in abundance, letters and diaries written by women. Unfortunately, the problem with many early diaries kept by women is that they seem rather ordinary and pedestrian, which is among the reasons early American diaries by women tended to be ignored by scholars. According to Margo Culley, author of *A Day at a Time: The Diary Literature of American Women from 1764 to the Present* (1993), many early American diarists regarded themselves as family and social historians, recording births, deaths, and community events with little commentary. It was not until the nineteenth century, as Culley points out, "that changing ideas of the self, influenced by romanticism, the industrial revolution, and the 'discovery' of the unconscious that diarists began to reveal their inner lives."

### *A Midwife's Tale*

In 1990, Laurel Thatcher Ulrich published *A Midwife's Tale: The Life of Martha Ballard, Based on Her Diary, 1785–1812.* The existence of Ballard's diary had long been known, but until Ulrich published her study, no scholar had considered it worthy of attention. In fact, many male scholars viewed Ballard's brief descriptions of labor and delivery, spinning and carding, and putting up vegetables as having little to do with the American past. Ulrich, in publishing the diary, made history and changed historians' attitudes toward such sources. *A Midwife's Tale* won a number of prizes, including the Pulitzer, was made into a film, and inspired a Web site entitled "Do History," where students can examine and interpret primary sources, including all 834 pages of Ballard's diary. (http://dohistory.org).

Ballard's diary is remarkable in a number of ways, not the least of which is the very detailed portrait it provides of daily life in colonial America. Ballard kept her diary for 27 years until just three weeks before her death at the age of 77. In modern terms, she would be referred to as a working mother in that she was not only a wife and the parent of nine children (six survived), but she was also a midwife who delivered more than 800 babies under incredibly difficult conditions—rising in the middle of the night, crossing rivers by canoe, and braving storms and rough terrain on horseback.

## The Goodness of Providence

As Ulrich notes, there are parts of Ballard's diary that rise to the level of lyricism. These parts are reminiscent of the sermons of her Puritan forbears and also of the later captivity narratives of women like Mary Rowlandson (1637–1711), who were held captive by Native Americans. Here is Ballard's's entry for April 24, 1789:

> **A sever Storm of rain. I was Calld at 1 hour pm from Mrs. Hussey's be Ebenzer Hewin. Crosst the river in their Boat. A great sea A going. We got safe over then sett out for Mr. Hewins. I Crost a stream on the way on fleeting Loggs & got safe over. Wonder full is the Goodness of providence. I then proceeded on my journey. Went beyond Mr Hainses & a Larg tree blew up by the roots before me which Caused my hors to sprin back & my life was spared. Great & marvillous are thy sparing mercies O God. I was assisted over the fallen tree by Mr. Hains. Went on. Soon Came to a stream. The Bridg was gone. Mr. Hewin took the rains waded thro & led the horse. Assisted by the same almighty power I got safe thro & arrivd unhurt. Mrs. Hewins safe delivd at 10 h Evn of a Daughter.**

Writers of Puritan sermons and captivity narratives were at great pains to see the hand of the deity in all aspects of their lives. Because of the concept of election—predestination to the afterlife—every good Puritan had to interpret disasters and near disasters as messages of their election or signs of the need for self-correction. If bad things happened, every devout Puritan considered the possibility that the ill luck was a message from the diety to change his or her direction. In many cases, especially in documents intended for public consumption, this tendency to see everything as having religious significance can eventually begin to feel forced (as it does in Mary Rowlandson's captivity narrative). In Ballard's diary, however, readers experience how such faith actually played out in real life. As Ulrich writes, "The religious language in Martha Ballard's diary strengthens the affinity with her Puritan progenitors. Dramatizing the dangers of her journey, she both glorified God and gave meaning and dimension to her own life . . . [these] religious sentiments become a kind of refrain, punctuating and accentuating each stage in the narrative. Such a passage reveals a storyteller, if not a writer, at work." Ballard's piety is unforced, natural, and a part of her everyday relation with the world.

## The Female Sphere

The parts of Ballard's diary that are less than literary are difficult to appreciate without Ulrich's careful guidance, but with her help, the diary presents a very different picture of early American life than what was portrayed in typical early, heroic literature—different even from the work of Bradstreet. There were two major spheres of existence in the early years of colonization: the male sphere and the female sphere. American literature and history tend to focus almost exclusively on the male sphere—exploring new land, hunting, leveling virgin forest, fighting natives, and as Mark Twain wrote in *The Adventures of Huckleberry Finn* of Huck's desire, "light[ing] out for the Territory ahead of the rest." Little attention is paid to the female sphere, except in the letters and diaries of women settlers.

Ballard's diary highlights the importance of women in the early years of the New Nation and showcases the true strength of female colonists. In her interpretation of Ballard's diary, Ulrich uses the weaving of cloth as a metaphor for how women became interwoven into a colonial economy dominated by the male sphere. As Ulrich writes, "The production of cloth wove a social web connecting women to one another and intersecting with the male economy."

It is hard to imagine the incredible effort that went into the production of cloth in the colonial era. Cloth was made from flax, cotton, or wool. Each material had to be first spun into thread and then woven into cloth. To turn flax into thread was, as Gail Collins notes in *America's Women: 400 Years of Dolls, Drudges, Helpmates, and Heroines* (2003), an "excruciating process in which the stalks were dried, combed, softened, cleaned, dried again, then 'broken' to separate the fibers, pounded, cleaned, and pounded again." Once transformed into thread, the thread itself had to be "treated with repeated washing, rinsing, bleaching, and beating" before it could be woven into cloth. When spinning wool, women used a large wheel that required them to move back and forth across the

**Mary Rowlandson**

Mary Rowlandson turned her eleven weeks of captivity by Native Americans during King Philip's War (1675–76) into an important work of early American nonfiction. Her captivity narrative, a scene from which is pictured in this nineteenth-century engraving, was very popular at the time of publication and went through four printings in one year.

room. In a full day of spinning, Collins notes, "a woman could walk as many as 20 miles." Women not only made and dyed cloth and fashioned it into clothing, but they also planted and tended kitchen gardens, made candles, beer, soap, and cheese, and preserved a variety of foods, in addition to cooking, cleaning, and raising their children.

If the typical hero of American literature was the solitary, independent man, women's lives were thus atypical in that they were deeply interdependent and communal, as Ballard's diary shows. The community of women in Ballard's town of Hallowell, Maine shared raw materials, baked goods, garden produce, and information. They worked together to spin, bake, clean, quilt, take care of the sick, and prepare the dead for burial. Thus, from a colonial woman's perspective, the great American novel would be Louisa May Alcott's *Little Women*, a story of community, not Mark Twain's *Huckleberry Finn*, a story about finding independence. Ulrich notes that the value of Ballard's diary lies not in heroics but in its very "dailiness":

> **To extract the river crossings without noting the cold days spent "footing" stockings, to abstract the births without recording the long autumns spent winding quills, pickling meat, and sorting cabbages, is to destroy the sinews of this earnest, steady, gentle, and courageous record. Martha sometimes slipped the folded half-sheets from which she constructed her diary into her bag when she crossed the river or waded through snow to sit out a tedious labor, and when she felt overwhelmed or enlivened by the very "trivia" the historians have dismissed, she said so, not in the soul-searching manner of a Puritan nor with the literary self-consciousness of a sentimentalist, but in a plain, matter-of-fact, and in the end unforgettable voice. For more than twenty-seven years, 9,965 days to be exact, she faithfully kept her record. Martha was not an introspective diarist, yet in this conscientious recording as much as in her occasional confessions, she revealed herself. "And now this year is come to a close," she wrote on December 31, 1800, "and happy is it if we have made a wise improvement of the time." For her, living was to be measured in doing. Nothing was trivial.**

## Seduced and Abandoned

In 1771, only five years after Ballard began her diary, Susanna Rowson published her novel of female seduction, *Charlotte Temple.*

Patterned on earlier British works, such as Samuel Richardson's *Pamela: Or, Virtue Rewarded* (1740) and *Clarissa: Or the History of a Young Lady* (1748), the novel warned young women about the consequences of losing one's "virtue." What is fascinating in *Charlotte Temple* is the gap between this fictional world and the reality of life recorded in Ballard's diary. As Ulrich notes, neither in Ballard's diary nor in other supporting materials is there any evidence "that in rural communities women who bore children out of wedlock were either ruined or abandoned as early novels would suggest." If, during her labor, an unmarried woman named the father of her child, her word was unquestioned, and the father had either to marry her or provide for the child's support. If the father decamped and lit out for the territories, the single mother generally continued to live with her family; most of these women eventually married. In fact, many women were pregnant when they married, and some families condoned premarital sex.

As a side note, it is interesting that Ballard's niece, Dorothy Barton, named two of her daughters after Richardson's novels: Pamela and Clarissa. Clarissa, later known as Clara Barton, followed in her aunt's footsteps by entering the medical field and would later found the American Red Cross.

## Midwifery

It is impossible to read *A Midwife's Tale*, of course, without learning a great deal about the practice of obstetrics in colonial America. Ballard lived and worked during a transitional time in American medicine when the old female-centered midwife culture was being supplanted by male doctors who considered themselves professionals. Through much of Ballard's life, birth was considered a domestic rather than a medical concern, and male doctors did not involve themselves in the birthing process unless there was a need for a surgical intervention. Doctors were called in to perform the gruesome task of dismembering a baby who had died before birth and was positioned in such a manner that the body could not easily be removed.

Midwifery, as practiced through much of the eighteenth century, worked with nature. Midwives did what they could to help mothers relax, but they tended not to interfere with what they regarded as a normal process. Doctors, on the other hand, when they began involving themselves in obstetrics, did tend to interfere, and their primary weapons were bloodletting, forceps, and the drug laudanum, a form of opium.

## CLARA BARTON AND THE AMERICAN RED CROSS

Clarissa Harlow Barton, later known as Clara Barton, was Martha Ballard's great-great niece. Some have speculated that a gift for healing must have run in the Ballard family, and that seems hard to deny when one notes that Ballard's great-great granddaughter, Mary Hobart, who preserved Ballard's diary and donated it to the Maine State Library, was graduated from the Woman's Medical College of the New York Infirmary in 1884, making her among the first women doctors in America.

Barton was born in 1821 in Oxford, Massachusetts. She began her career as a teacher at a very early age and eventually founded her own school in New Jersey. The school was quite successful, but when the board of directors passed her over and hired a man to head the school, Barton left in disgust. In 1861, she was hired as a clerk in the U.S. Patent Office in Washington, D.C., the first woman to hold such a clerkship in the federal government.

While working in Washington during the Civil War (1861–1865), Barton learned that many soldiers died not from lack of medical attention but from lack of supplies. As a result, she began to solicit donations and established an organization to distribute the donated goods. U.S. Surgeon General William A. Hammond gave her a special pass that allowed her to travel along with army ambulances "for the purpose of distributing comforts for the sick and wounded, and nursing them." Barton traveled throughout Virginia and in parts of South Carolina for three years and earned the nickname "Angel of the battlefield."

In 1869, during a trip to Geneva, Switzerland, Barton learned about the Red Cross. As she explained herself in an open letter to the American people, the Red Cross is:

> *A confederation of Relief Societies in different countries, acting under the Geneva Convention, [that] carries on its work under the sign of the Red Cross. The aim of these societies is to ameliorate the condition of wounded soldiers in the armies in campaign on land or sea, and to furnish relief in cases of great national calamity.*

At the time of Barton's visit to Geneva, the United States had not signed the treaty. While in Europe, Barton volunteered to work for the International Red Cross. In 1877, IRC authorities asked her to establish an American Red Cross, which she headed for 23 years until her retirement in 1904 at the age of 82.

**Clara Barton**
Clara Barton, great niece of Martha Ballard and founder of the American Red Cross, seems to have shared some of Ballard's courage and spirit. She got permission to go behind the battlelines to nurse wounded Union soldiers in 1862 and served during some of the most desperately fought campaigns of the Civil War.

### Bloodletting

As a midwife, Martha Ballard not only delivered babies, she also treated the sick. In most cases, her folk and herbal remedies were sufficient to restore health—or at least they did no harm as the patient recovered on his or her own. However, if the patient did not respond to Ballard's treatment and had the wherewithal to pay, then one of the local doctors might be called in. While colonial doctors and midwives shared many medical practices, doctors had a tendency to be much more invasive than midwives; for example, doctors used forceps during difficult deliveries. In addition, doctors often relied on the practice of bloodletting. Bloodletting has ancient roots; it may be, in fact, one of the most ancient of all medical practices. The word "plethora," which means profusion or abundance, originally referred to the condition of having too much blood, which was thought to cause illness. Ancient physicians may have modeled bloodletting on the natural process of menstruation.

In the medieval period, bloodletting, while recommended by physicians, was generally performed by barber surgeons. The symbol of the barber pole, in fact, refers to the practice of bloodletting. The original pole had a basin at the top and bottom, representing the bowls holding the leeches, or bloodsucking worms, and into which the blood flowed. The pole represented the staff that the patient held to encourage blood flow. The red stripe on the pole represented blood, while the white represented the tourniquet the barber used to help the veins stand out.

Bloodletting was used to treat almost every imaginable illness from indigestion to cancer; Ballard even mentions its use during childbirth. The doctor or barber used leeches or surgical instruments to bleed patients, taking as much as four pints of blood at a time. Although used for centuries, the practice of bloodletting was taken to ridiculous heights in the eighteenth and nineteenth centuries. Many people believe that America's first president, George Washington, actually died from the practice. He was bled to treat a throat infection, being drained of nine pints of blood in a 24-hour period.

Ballard had an exemplary record as a midwife. In a period when many women died during childbirth, she saw to the delivery of nearly 1,000 babies without losing a single patient. Only five of her patients died subsequent to delivery. Fourteen babies were stillborn, and five died within an hour or two of delivery. According to Ulrich:

> By our standards, mortality was high. Martha saw one maternal death for every 198 living births. Today that rate is one per 10,000. But as late as 1930, there was one maternal death for every 150 births in the United States; the major gains in obstetrical safety have come in the past fifty years. In fact, many historians believe that the routine employment of physicians in the nineteenth century probably increased rather than decreased mortality. Records of an early nineteenth-century New Hampshire physician, whose case load was almost identical to Martha Ballard's, shows higher stillbirth rations and four maternal deaths at delivery . . . What is even more striking is the large number of complications recorded in his records . . . [Moreover] dangers did not decrease as hospital delivery became more common.

These facts put into perspective the dread with which many women in colonial America faced childbirth. Many letter writers and diarists expressed their fear of dying in childbirth, as did Anne Bradstreet. In "Before the Birth of One of Her Children," Bradstreet wrote to her husband: "How soon, my Dear, death may my steps attend, How soon't may be thy lot to lose they friend." Although doctors later began to malign midwives as ignorant, dirty, and dangerous, Ballard seemed to have had the respect of most of the doctors she worked with. In fact, she was invited at least four times by local doctors to witness "dissections"—similar to modern autopsies—evidence that they considered her a valuable colleague.

Whereas most of Ballard's patients and their babies survived—at least through the lying-in period—many women did die during childbirth or suffered the loss of several children. One notable diarist, Mary Vial Holyoke, bore 12 children, of which only three survived to adulthood, despite the fact that her husband was a prominent doctor in Salem, Massachusetts. Seven of her children died either at birth or in infancy. The entries in her diary, though terse, reflect the grief mothers felt at losing their children: "My Dear Polly died."

Ulrich speculates that it was a woman like Ballard who was the inspiration for Sarah Orne Jewett's (1849–1909) character Mrs. Todd in *The Country of the Pointed Firs* (1910), as well as for Sarah Josepha Hale's (1788–1879) Mrs. Watson in *Northwood* (1827). Perhaps many New England towns and villages each had their own Martha Ballard—housewife, healer, herbalist, and good neighbor.

## Early to Rise

Ballard's diary also sheds light on the work of two other American writers: Benjamin Franklin and J. Hector St. John de Crèvecoeur (1735–1813). One of the major strands in Franklin's writing, derived from his Puritan forebears, is his strong sense of the importance of duty and hard work. It was Franklin, after all, who said, "Early to bed and early to rise, makes a man healthy, wealthy, and wise," and he could hardly have had a better model of the sort of work ethic he believed in than Ballard. Almost any passage from her diary gives one a sense of how hard she worked:

> **I was Calld from Mrs Moore to Steven Hinkleys wife at 10 hour morning. Shee was delivered at 11 of a son. I part drest the infant and was Calld to return to Mrs. Moore. Find her more unwell. Shee was delivered at 4 hour 30 minutes of a son. The Children were the first Born of their mamys. I returned home at 8 hour Evening. Brother Ebenezer Moore sleeps here. I made Bids, washt dishes, swept house, and got supper. I feel some fatigud.**

At the writing of the above passage, Ballard was 61 years old. Simply traveling from place to place in mid-winter (this passage was written in January 1796) took a tremendous effort. Washing dishes involved fetching and heating water, and getting supper also required many more steps than such a job does today—trips to the root cellar, tending the fire, and so on. Although Ballard cannot be said to be entirely uncomplaining, her sense of duty clearly is one of her defining characteristics.

On the other hand, Ballard's diary makes a telling contrast to St. John de Crèvecoeur's *Letter's from an American Farmer* (1782). His "Wife," whom he capitalizes but never names (Mehitable Tippet) worked from dawn to dusk, as Ballard did, and ran the farm while her husband was away. In the end, she was murdered by Indians. Although St. John de Crèvecoeur romanticized the life of a gentleman farmer in America, Mehitable herself stands as a major correction to his idealization.

## Growing Old in America

Bradstreet wrote this about aging:

> **My memory is short, and braine is dry.**
> **My Almond-tree (gray haires) doth flourish now,**

> And back, once straight, begins apace to bow.
> My grinders now are few, my sight doth faile
> My skin is wrinkled, and my cheeks are pale.
> No more rejoice, at musickes pleasant noise.

Growing old in New England was a distinct possibility for many people because it had not been stricken by disease, as in Europe, and was not in the southern colonies. Ballard lived to be 77, and her husband, Ephraim, lived well into his 90s. Although mortality statistics were not kept in any systematic way in the colonial period, it seems that the climate in New England was conducive to long life, and the lack of crowded cities curbed the progress of contagious diseases, allowing many to survive even the worst epidemics of smallpox and yellow fever.

## Tyranny

When Abigail Adams enjoined her husband in 1776 to "remember the ladies," her major concern was the tyranny that husbands have over their wives. She worried that "all men would be tyrants if they could." Obviously, Adams chose her words carefully, borrowing a term from the *Declaration of Independence* (1776), which accuses "the present King of Great Britain . . . [of] having in direct object the establishment of an absolute Tyranny" over the colonies. She clearly hoped that the men who so hated political tyranny would also abolish the domestic version. However, John Adams ignored his wife, and American women were not freed from the tyranny of their husbands for many years.

### Women Without Rights

The nature of the power that colonial husbands could hold over their wives was nearly absolute. Whereas single women and widows had some level of freedom and independence, a married woman's legal identity was erased when she got married. According to historian Carol Berkin in *First Generations: Women in Colonial America* (1996):

> . . . under English common law, women were legal persons only if they reached their majority and did not marry. As *femme sole*, or woman alone, a free Englishwoman could sue and be sued, make contracts, earn and pay wages, own and sell property in her lifetime, and will it to her chosen heirs upon her death. Marriage—which was the primary ritual of adulthood for

> a woman—converted her to *femme covert*, or woman covered, enforcing the exchange of her legal persona for the protection and support of her husband. In its most pristine and extreme interpretation, the law denied married women the right to make judgments regarding their own economic circumstances. It muted their voice in the courts, restricted their accumulation and dispersement of material wealth, and made them less than responsible for their misdeeds or achievements in the public sphere. A woman was a legal incompetent, as children, idiots, and criminals were under English law. As femme covert she was stripped of all property; once married the clothes on her back, her personal possessions . . . and even her body became her husband's, to direct, to manage, and to use.

Most husbands did not allow themselves to be corrupted by this level of power, and many husbands and wives lived in harmony and equality. However, this was not always the case, and Adams was right to be concerned that some men would abuse their power over their wives.

## The Diary of Nancy Shippen Livingston

In her diary, Nancy Shippen Livingston (1763–1841) tells the tale of her unhappy marriage and what happens to her when she chooses to leave her husband. Livingston was a member of one of America's most prominent families. Her mother was a part of the political Lee family of Virginia and her father a Philadelphia physician. In 1779, when Nancy was just 16, she married Henry Beekman Livingston, the heir to a large fortune. Although she was in love with another man, Nancy married Livingston to please her parents. She soon discovered that her husband had multiple affairs and several illegitimate children, not to mention a jealous temper. Pregnant, she left her husband and returned to her parents' home. Soon after the birth of her child, her husband began pressuring her to give the child to his mother to rear. Knowing that she had no legal right to the child and further pressured by her father, who was worried the child would be disinherited, Livingston gave her daughter, Peggy, to her mother-in-law. Nine months later, on her first visit to the child, Peggy did not recognize her mother:

> I beg'd her to come [to] me & call'd her my darling Child & try'd to take her, by force. All woul'd not do, she wou'd not take ye least notice of me, not let me take her from her grandmother;

> **it was more than I cou'd bear, I was distress'd and mortified, & burst into a flood of tears.**

In 1789, when Livingston threatened to divorce Henry, he, in turn, threatened to take custody of the child from his mother and move her far away. It was not until Peggy was 16 that she was allowed to live with her mother. Even before she relinquished custody of Peggy, Livingston wrote advice to her infant daughter about the nature of feminine reality in colonial America:

> **[Men] are naturally tyrannical; they will have pleasures & liberty, yet insist that Women renounce both: do not examine whether their rights are well founded; let it suffice to you that they are established; They are masters, we have only to suffer & obey with a good grace.**

This was exactly the kind of tyranny that Adams had feared.

## The Memoir of Abigail Abbot Bailey

Even Adams could not have imagined what some women suffered at the hands of their husbands. Abigail Abbot Bailey's story is not a common one, but it certainly fits Adams's definition of "absolute tyranny." Abigail was born in 1746 and married Asa Bailey at the age of 22, a fairly advanced age for brides of that era. The couple settled in New Hampshire, and she bore Asa 17 children. Her memoir, found by a friend after her death, was edited for publication because he felt it would make an instructive biography. Margo Culley writes that Bailey's diary is "in the tradition of women's religious autobiography as well as in the tradition of American 'captivity narratives.'"

After Bailey had been married for about 20 years, she noted that "Mr. B. began to behave in a very uncommon manner." Asa eventually disclosed that he had decided to uproot the family and move to Ohio. Bailey, unhappy with his decision, acquiesced because it was her duty to obey her husband. He then outlined his plans to the older children who were also unhappy but obedient. At first, Bailey says she did not really understand what her husband was up to:

> **All this pretended plan was but a specious cover to infernal designs. Here I might pause, and wonder, and be silent, humble, and astonished, as long as I live! A family, which God had**

> committed to my head and husband, as well as to me, to protect and train up for God, must now have their peace and honor sacrificed by an inhuman parent, under the most subtle and vile intrigues, to gratifiy the most contemptible passion! I had before endured sorrowful days and years, on account of the follies, cruelties, and base incontinency of him who vowed to be my faithful husband. But all past afflictions vanish before those which follow.

Clearly, Bailey's husband was planning something much worse than moving his family west. As she tells it, "He now commenced a new series of conduct in relation to [one of their daughters]" in order to convince her to accompany him on his initial trip west. Bailey started to believe that her husband had sexual designs on their daughter, but she could not bring herself to believe that such a thing was possible:

> Though all the conduct of Mr. B. from day to day, seemed to demonstrate my apprehension, that he was determined, and was continually plotting, to ruin this poor young daughter, yet it was so intolerably crossing to every feeling of my soul to admit such a thought, that I strove with all my might to banish it from my mind, and to disbelieve the possibility of such a thing.

Bailey notes that her daughter was frightened by her father's behavior, yet, fearful and confused, said nothing. She also notes that her husband was irrationally brutal with this girl, beating her without cause.

After nearly two years of suspecting sexual abuse, Bailey finally gathered enough evidence of her husband's wicked behavior to ask for a divorce. He then convinced her that, as part of the property settlement, she must accompany him to New York. After they arrived in New York, he told Bailey that the laws there were different and she no longer had any rights. He then proceeded to abandon her there. Alone and virtually penniless, Bailey determined to return home and confront her husband. She managed to acquire a horse and made the nearly 300-mile journey by herself. With the help of her brothers, she was able to divorce Asa in 1793.

Bailey, like Mary Rowlandson, peppers her tale of horror with evidence of her faith and trust in God, despite the terrors of what happened to her and her daughter. Even at the point of her final split with her husband, she was at pains to show an upright religious spirit:

> I earnestly entreated him to break off his sins by unfeigned repentance, and make it his immediate care to become reconciled to God through Jesus Christ, who died for lost man, and even for the greatest of sinners.

## Pestilence

Before she began the diary that has survived, Ballard lived through an epidemic of dysentery in which three of her children died. Abigail Adams herself fell ill with dysentery during an epidemic in Braintree, Massachusetts, in 1775, during which her mother and John's brother, Elihu, died. She wrote to John, "Such is the distress of the neighborhood that I can scarcely find a well person to assist me in looking after the sick. So mortal a time the oldest man does not remember."

### The Diaries of Elizabeth Sandwich Drinker

Like the English diarist Samuel Pepys (1633–1703), who wrote in his famous diary of the bubonic plague that struck London in 1665, Elizabeth Sandwich Drinker (1735–1807), a wealthy Quaker living in Philadelphia, who is well known for her diary entries during the Revolutionary War, detailed the horrors of the yellow fever epidemic that struck Philadelphia in 1793. Although epidemics were by no means rare in colonial America, yellow fever was considered primarily a tropical disease and, thus, unexpected in Philadelphia. Yellow fever, in fact, is carried by a variety of mosquito, which, unlike other varieties, prefers an urban to a rural environment and lays its eggs in clean standing water and cisterns, although doctors of the era had no idea what caused the disease. A "perfect storm" of events combined to create the ideal climate for the spread of this awful illness. The summer had been dry and hot, and water levels were dangerously low. As a result of political upheaval in the Caribbean, thousands of refugees from that tropical region arrived in Philadelphia. Soon, people began to die of a mysterious ailment that was eventually identified as the yellow fever. According to writer Bob Arnebeck, in "A Short History of Yellow Fever in the US":

> The most insidious [symptom of yellow fever] was the conviction of the victim that he was getting well. The fever had a remission two to three days after the on-set of symptoms of nausea and general debility which sent some victims back to their jobs and into the streets only to drop dead. As the disease matured

> so did the horror of the symptoms. There could be bleeding at any and every orifice of the body, even through the pores of the skin. Vomit came out black. There could be constant hiccupping so that relatively lucid moments provided no comfort. Not a few fevers course their way through the body seemingly capricious in the pain they inflict. Yellow fever did so with uncommon destructiveness of bodily functions.

Dr. Benjamin Rush, well-known for his writings on education and his courageous battle to convince people of the benefits of inoculation against smallpox, worked hard to determine the cause of this devastating disease and to help treat its victims. He developed a "cure" that involved copious bleeding and treatment with a tincture of mercury, and he believed the cure worked because he used in on himself. He notes in his diary:

> On the 9th of October . . . toward evening, I was seized with a pain in the back. . . . About 12:00, I awoke with a chilly fit. A violent fever followed. At 1:00, I called for Mr. Fisher [his pupil]. . . . He bled me plentifully and gave me a dose of the mercurial medicine. . . . In the morning, the medicine operated kindly, and my fever abated. In the afternoon, it returned. . . . Mr. Fisher bled me again. . . . The next day, the fever left me, but in so weak a state that I awoke two successive nights with a faintness which threatened the extinction of my life. . . . My convalescence was extremely slow.

Unfortunately, Rush was simply one of those who survived the fever, and his cure probably did more harm than good.

The statistics of the epidemic are quite frightening. More than a third of Philadelphia's population of about 50,000 left the city during the epidemic; Drinker was one of them. About 4,000 people died, including ten of the doctors who had remained to treat the sick. Eventually, Rush was one of only three doctors left to treat some 6,000 cases of yellow fever.

Drinker stayed in her country home throughout the epidemic, but her husband and others traveled back and forth from the city to report the increasingly grim news of death and destruction. She records the first death on July 25 and notes on August 16, "`Tis a sickly time now in Philada and there has been an unusual number of funerals there lately." On August 23, she reports:

> A Fever prevails in the City . . . of ye malignant kind; numbers have died of it. Some say it was occasioned by damaged Coffee and Fish . . . others say it was imported in a Vessel from Cape Francois . . . 'Tis really an alarming and serious time.

In attributing the fever to rotting coffee, Drinker is referring to Rush's theory of the origin of the fever.

By August 27, Drinker is aware that the fever is yellow fever and notes that some have "burnt Tar in ye streets" in an attempt to drive the illness away. Sounding a bit like Bradstreet when her home was burnt to the ground, Drinker worries, "Our House is left, filled with valuables, nobody to take care of it—ye Grapevines hanging in clusters, and some of ye fruit trees loaded." However, she quickly puts her worries into perspective when she writes, "those are matters of little consequence."

As the pestilence grows, the rites and rituals of burial are sacrificed to expediency. On September 10, Drinker notes, "We have also heard today that the dead are put into their Coffins just as they die, without changing their clothes, or laying out; and are buried in a hour or two after their disease." By September 12, she says, "two or three dead bodies were thrown into Friends' burying ground, over ye wall." Just a couple of days later she notes, "W. Sansom is near his end . . . his coffin is bespoke, and his grave dug, a common thing now." On October 4, she notes, "The accounts from ye City this day, seem to be worse than they have yet been. We were informed that dead bodies have been found in some houses in the City, who have been forsaken in their illness, and not discovered for some days after death."

Interestingly, Drinker seems to have identified an important factor in the spread of the disease—temperature. She writes on October 5, "To day 'tis said there is an alteration for the better. This has been a fine, clear, cool day. I have remarked 2 or 3 times, when he have heard of an abatement of ye disease, the weather was cool." Unfortunately, the weather warmed again soon after, causing an upsurge in deaths.

Day after day, Drinker records the dead by name, people she knew and those she only knew of. She is grateful that her family is well, "Tho' bodily weakness is experienced by some of our family, we have great cause for thankfulness." For the first time since July, Drinker notes on October 17, "we have not heard this evening of any deaths." On November 3, Drinker quotes from the *Federal Gazette:*

> **It gives great pleasure of the Editor to hear, from every quarter of our City, that universal health prevails in a degree equal to any former period in the history of this country.**

Drinker made daily entries in her diary for nearly 50 years, from 1758 when she was 23 years old until the year of her death in 1807. It is an invaluable resource to anyone who wants to understand women's lives in the period and some of the most important events in American history. Drinker, a Quaker who opposed the Revolution—and war in general—provides a detailed picture of Philadelphia during the war from a point of view quite different from most historical accounts, which are, as the saying goes, usually written by the winners.

## Another Abigail

*The Letters of Abigaill Levy Franks, 1733–1748* are, according to her editor, Yale University's Edith B. Gelles:

> **the earliest known corpus of letters by a Jewish woman anywhere in Europe's western colonies.**

Unlike the works of some of the other colonial women writers discussed in this chapter, Franks's letters were known and used by historians before they were collected by Gelles in 2004.

Franks's description of New York colonial politics, and in particular a court fight initiated by the colony's governor, William Cosby, in the 1730s, have been often cited. As Gelles says, "Because of the vagaries of source survival, no other documentation exists, or has yet been discovered, that describes from a more or less neutral perspective some of the factional attitudes amongt the principal actors of this dispute." Nevertheless, the entire body of Franks's letters were not generally available to the public until the publication of Gelles's book, which contains 35 letters that Franks wrote to her son Napthali from 1733, when the 17-year-old boy sailed for England to work for his uncles, until 1748.

No record exists of Franks's birth or death, although the dates are known. Bilhah Abigaill Levy was born in London, England in 1696 to a large and wealthy Jewish MERCANTILE family. Her father,

### Ye Olde New York

**When the Levy family—Moses, Richea, Abigaill, and Asher—arrived in New York City from London in 1703, they certainly would have experienced culture shock. Whereas London was a great cosmopolitan city at the time, New York was a mere colonial outpost. Of the 5,000 residents, only about 250 were Jewish. Jews, however, were not the only minority group in New York, which then may have been the most multicultural of all the colonies.**

**New York had been a Dutch colony before it was taken over by the British in 1664, and many Dutch settlers remained when the Levy family arrived. Because it was a port city, New York was also home to numerous ethnic and religious groups—for example, French Huguenots, Germans, Swedes, Scots, Irish, and people from the West Indies.**

**Despite the relatively small population, New York was crowded because most people lived in one area on lower Manhattan. People were even encouraged to purchase inexpensive underwater property along the East River with the expectation that purchasers would fill in the water with soil and reclaim the land. Because of the danger of fire, most houses were built of brick, and they were constructed very close together. When the Levy family arrived, there were no public schools, no hospitals, and no workhouses to help deal with the city's poor. All of those institutions arose during Abigaill Franks's lifetime. Most streets were unpaved, and open sewers ran along the middle of the street. Pigs ran free throughout the city.**

**New York's neighborhoods tended to form around ethnic groups. The "Dock Ward," for example, was primarily Jewish, but both rich and poor lived in close proximity. Not until after the American Revolution did neighborhoods begin to form around socio-economic classes.**

Moses Levy, his wife Richea, and their two children, Abigaill and Asher, immigrated to New York City in 1703.

After their arrival, three other boys were born to the family. It is not known exactly how Abigaill Franks was educated, but she clearly received the same educational advantages as her brothers, probably by private tutor. Gelles notes that Franks's education was "atypical for an early eighteenth-century woman." She adds that in the correspondence among Franks and her brothers Asher and Nathan, "the three siblings demonstrate unusually cultivated and compatible intellects as adults." In her education and sophistication, Franks is different from some of the other women writers profiled in this chapter and more like the other Abigail, Mrs. John Adams.

Franks's mother died when she was eleven, and she became mother to her younger brothers until her father remarried to Grace Mears, with whom he had seven more children. Franks did not like her stepmother, and Gelles speculates that Franks may have married young (she was 16, young for a Jewish woman of the day) to escape from a family life that was no longer congenial. Abigaill married Isaac Franks, an apprentice of her father's, also a Jewish immigrant from England. With Isaac, who was eight years older, she had nine children, two of whom died young. The family was prosperous, had servants, and may even have owned a slave.

## Letters of Advice

Franks's letters to her son Napthali were written from a sense of both duty and affection. She makes no bones about the fact that she does not like to write, "I have very often designed to answer A Letter As Soon received In order to have Some method, but As I hate write[in]g, I Cant Perswade my Self to take Soe much time." She never recopies, so, as she herself says, her letters are often afflicted with blots, and her spelling is nothing if not inventive. Although Abigail Adams was always concerned about her spelling, Franks does not seem to be. Still, she often makes excuses for the appearance of her letters: "My Pen is Very bad & soe is my Spectacles and Late at Night, for I never write none of my Letters but at Night, for thats the Only time I have to be alone."

In another letter she writes:

> **When I write you Such Long Letters, you must Overlook ye blunders & scrawls, for I hate writing & allways write in haste.**

Nevertheless, duty is bred in Franks's bones and as much as she counsels her son in his various duties, she holds herself to the same standards. In a letter from 1734, in fact, she rejoices in what she sees as her son's dutifulness. "Nothing in Life can be fore gratefull then to hear that you Dischage your duty to y[ou]r Relations and your Self in so Agreeable And Aproved of a manner."

In fact Franks's letters are packed with advice to Napthali, whom she always addresses as Heartsey, which may be derived from the Yiddish for "dear heart." Although Heartsey is 17 when the letters begin and 32 when they end, Franks seems to still see him as a young man, advising him and criticizing his behavior. Some of the advice is of the nature of Shakespeare's Polonius to his son Laertes, "To thine own self be true." For example, Franks tells Napthali, "All my Wishes are Centered in the honourable & Gratefull discharge of your duty in all Respects, and Even in that I have no fears, being you have made Soe happy a beginning in having y[ou]r Conduct Approved of by all y[ou]r Friends, and as the Coppy [meaning here unclear] says, a good beginning Makes a good End. I hope it may always be y[ou] Fortune in whthever Station of Life you may be Throw'n into."

Although some of her advice to her son is of this tenor, much is down to earth and practical. In a letter written in the year her son left home, Franks tells him:

> **I Observe You Give me an Acc[oun]t of how you Spend your time, I find noe fault in it but your not taking more time for your Studying of books, for If you don't doe it now, you will hardly fallow it when you grow oulder and will have an Excuse that buissness is a hindrance. My advice Should be that two mornings in a Week Should be intirly Untill diner time Dedicated to Some Usefull book, besides an hour Every morning throughout the Year to the Same Purpose.**

## Letters of Criticisms

Franks is also quick to criticize Naphtali if he fails to live up to her expectations, which he frequently does by neglecting to write. She often complains not on her own but on her husband's behalf. In a letter written in 1740, she calls his failure to write "unpardonable" and adds that she will not continue to reproach him because she is sure his father will do the job thoroughly. He is also chastised for failing to send items she has requested, failing to properly distribute the pickles and other edibiles that she sends to him, and neglecting to convey her greetings to family members as she has requested. She chides him for not givng Mrs. Salomons the "Cagg [keg of peppers] I sent her" and adds these things are quite wrong. Her direct, no-nonsense style is evident in this complaint she writes to Naphtali in 1741, as is her willingness to use guilt to goad her son into action:

> **I wish the Multiplicity of y[ou]r Affairs would have premited you to have Sent the box I beg'd Soe Earnestly for, but I find if I Am not to be disappointed, I must Apply to Mrs. Salomons. I find Her**

> **to be the Only person your side of the Watter that is willing to Oblige, for You too Frequently Neglect Sending ye Triffles I Write for, wich I could instance in Many things. Therefore, whenever I Send for any Thing, I Never Speak of it that noe One may know my Disappointment but my Self.**

## Observations

Franks's clear-eyed observations of the characters of the people she writes about are as blunt as her criticisms. The ladies of her synagogue are "a Stupid Set of people." Her nephew Colly is "neither Ruled in his Passions by right nor reason." Of an acquaintance she says her "Very Disagre[eable]" life is "owing to her Implacable Temper"; of another acquaintance she says, "She is a base Vile woman and her Actions has Allways bin of a Piece, tho' I think in this Last Affaire She has Outdon her Ussal Outdoings of malice and Craft."

Franks's intelligence is clear not only in her wit but also in her taste in literature, which is that of a cosmopolitan and sophisticated woman. She is as reluctant to suffer bad writing as she is to suffer fools, and she writes to her son that she consigned a "trashy" novel he sent her to the fire. Although she occasionally asks Natphali to send snuff boxes and coal grates from London, she most frequently requests books and journals, and her letters are nicely salted with quotations from what she has read. She liked Addison, Pope, Smollet, Dryden, and Fielding and was, as Gelles says, "modern and secular in thought and taste—a daughter of the emerging Enlightenment." Franks tells her son that if she had the freedom to do so, she would happily spend:

> **. . . three hours of the 24 from my Family Affairs to be diping in a good Author And relinquish Every other Gaity Commonly Called the Pleassure of Life.**

## Literature and Religion in a Secular Culture

Over the years, Franks asks Napthali to send, among other things, a ballad farce by Henry Cary called *The Honest Yorkshireman*; Pierre Massuet's history of the Polish kings; *Hibernicus Letters or a Philosophical Miscellany* by James Arbuckle; and the *Polite Philosopher* by James Forrester. Franks was also an avid reader of the *Gentleman's Magazine*, which Gelles describes as being the eighteenth-century version of the modern literary magazine *The New Yorker*.

That Franks was a woman of the ENLIGHTENMENT is clear not only in her taste in literature but also in her attitude toward religion. There is very little mention of Judiaism in Franks's letters, and, Gelles notes, the comments Franks does make are "explicitly derogatory." At the same time that she reminds Napthali to say his prayers and avoid foods inconsistent with a kosher diet, she tells him that she wishes for a Calvin or Luther to reform Judaism and rid it of "idle cerimonies" and superstitions. According to Gelles, "What distinguishes Abigaill's letters from other early American women's writing is her irreverence, her lack of piety as well as literary pretentions."

Franks's secularism was put to the test by her children's choice of spouses. Although Napthali pleased her by marrying his cousin Phila, her daughter (also Phila) broke her heart by marrying outside of their religion. Phila not only married a wealthy Christian, but she also eloped a full six months before she told her parents of the union. Reading Franks's letters up to this point, one might think that she would not mind if her children assimilated into the larger culture by marrying Christians, but Franks's Judaism is affirmed by her profound grief over her daughter's behavior. She tells Napthali, "I am now retired from Town and would from my Self (if it Where Possiable to have Some peace of mind) from the Severe Affliction I am Under on the Conduct of that Unhappy Girle." She is devasted by Phila's deception as much as by her choice of partners, especially after she had so often said, "noe Consideration in Life should Ever Induce her to Disoblige Such good parents." Frank wishes never to see her daughter or son-in-law again, though she says her maternal instincts force her to wish the girl well. She later tells Napthali that her "Spirets is too Depressed to write" to other family members and asks him to apologize for her.

Although Franks was secular in her approach to life, and although she seldom mentions her religion in her many letters, Judaism was central to her being. She believed she had raised her children right and that they would not stray. In this she was disappointed. As it turns out, none of her grandchildren were raised as Jews, not even Napthali's children.

Abigaill Franks adds another voice to the chorus of colonial women who left detailed records in letters and diaries. Hers is distinct, and different in many ways, but it belongs with the others to the story that is American culture.

## Timeline

| Science, Technology, and the Arts | Literature | History |
|---|---|---|
| **1485** Botticelli *The Birth of Venus* | | |
| **1492** | | Columbus discovers America |
| **1497** | | John Cabot explores the Atlantic coast of Canada |
| **1499** | | Amerigo Vespucci first sees the coast of South America |
| **1500** Dürer *Self-Portrait* | | |
| **1503–05** Da Vinci *Mona Lisa* | | |
| **1505** Raphael *Madonna and Child* | | las Casas petitions Spanish Crown on behalf of Native Americans |
| **1507** | | The name "America" is first used in a geography book |
| **1512** del Sarto *The Annunciation* | | |
| **1519** | Cortez *First Letter from Mexico to the Spanish Crown* | Cortez conquers Aztecs in Mexico |
| **1530** Holbein *Thomas Howard Prince of Norfolk* | | |
| **1541** Michaelangelo completes *The Last Judgement* | | Coronado explores in Texas |
| **1542** Titian *St. John the Baptist* | | |
| **1543** Copernicus *On the Revolution of the Heavenly Bodies* | | |
| **1552** | las Casas *The Very Brief Relation of the Devastation of the Indies* | |
| **1565** | | The first permanent European colony in North America is founded at St. Augustine |
| **1568** Bruegel *The Peasant Dance* | | |
| **1586** El Greco *The Burial of Count Orgaz* | | Settlement at Roanoke, Virginia |
| **1587** | | The first English child, Virginia Dare, is born in Roanoke |
| **1588** | Harriot *A Brief and True Report of the New Found Land of Virginia* | |

| Science, Technology, and the Arts | Literature | History |
|---|---|---|
| **1598** First opera, Jacopo Peri's *Dafne,* produced | | |
| **1600** Gilbert *De Magnete,* [*On Magnetism*] | | |
| **1604** Galileo builds telescope; discovers craters and mountains on the moon; Kepler publishes laws of planetary motion | | |
| **1605** Rubens *The Fall of Phaeton* | Smith *A Description of New England* | |
| **1607** | | Settlement at Jamestown |
| **1609** Native tobacco is first planted and harvested in Virginia by colonists | | |
| **1619** | | First slaves brought to America |
| **1620** Bacon *Novum Organum (or True Directions Concerning the Interpretation of Nature)* | | |
| **1621** | | First Thanksgiving |
| **1628** Harvey *On the Motion of the Heart* | | Morton celebrates May Day at Merry Mount |
| **1630** | Winthrop *A Model of Christian Charity* | |
| **1636** Van Dyke *Mary Princess Royal, and William, Prince of Orange* | Morton *New English Canaan* | Williams founds Providence Rhode Island; Anne Hutchinson banished from Massachusetts Bay<br>Harvard College founded |
| **1637** Descartes *Geometry* | | |
| **1639** | *Freeman's Oath* | |
| **1640** | *Bay Psalm Book* first published | |
| **1642** Pascal invents the mechanical adding machine;<br>Rembrandt *The Night Watch* | Williams *A Key into the Languages of America*<br>Bradstreet *The Tenth Muse Lately Sprung Up in America* | Publication of the *Cambridge Platform* |
| **1660** | | Quaker missionary Mary Dyer hanged in Boston<br>Dutch surrender New Amsterdam to British; renamed New York |
| **1662** | Wigglesworth *Day of Doom* | |

| Year | Science, Technology, and the Arts | Literature | History |
|---|---|---|---|
| **1666** | First signed Stradivarius violin | Danforth *A Brief Recognition of New England's Errand into the Wilderness* | |
| **1676** | | | King Philip's War<br>Pennsylvania founded |
| **1682** | | Rowlandson *The Sovereignty and Goodness of God* | Massachusetts Bay Charter revoked |
| **1685** | | Mather *Memorable Providences Relating to Witchcraft and Possession* | |
| **1687** | Newton *Principia Mathematica* | | |
| **1689** | Purcell's opera *Dido and Aeneas,* produced | | |
| **1690** | | Locke *Essay Concerning Human Understanding* | Salem witchcraft trials |
| **1692** | | Sewell *The Selling of Joseph* | |
| **1696** | | Birth of Abigaill Levy Franks<br>Cook *The Sot-Weed Factor* | |
| **1700** | | Franklin *The Dogood Papers* | |
| **1701** | | | Smallpox epidemic in Boston; first use of inoculation in America<br>Yale College founded |
| **1702** | | Mather *Magnalia Christi Americana* | |
| **1704** | | First enduring newspaper in America, *The Boston News-Letter*, is published | |
| **1718** | | | New Orleans founded by the French |
| **1725** | Vivaldi *Four Seasons* | Franklin *Poor Richard's Almanac* | |
| **1728** | | Edwards *Sinners in the Hands of an Angry God* | Jewish colonists in New York City build the first American synagogue |
| **1730** | First art show in colonies, organized by John Smibert | | |
| **1732** | | | Birth of George Washington<br>Georgia founded |
| **1735** | | Birth of Martha Ballard | John Peter Zenger tried for libel |
| **1737** | First copper colonial coins minted | | |

| Science, Technology, and the Arts | Literature | History |
|---|---|---|
| **1742** Handel's *Messiah* premiers | Rousseau *The Social Contract* | Beginning of French and Indian War |
| **1743** Franklin founds the American Philosophical Society | | |
| **1733–48** | Levy Franks *Letters* | |
| **1764** Hargreaves invents the spinning jenny | Dickinson *Letters from a Farmer in Pennsylvania* | Stamp Act |
| | | Boston Massacre |
| **1766** | Rogers *Ponteach* | Boston Tea Party |
| **1769** Watt invents the steam engine | Wheatley *Poems on Various Subjects* | |
| | Warren *The Group* | |
| | Paine *Common Sense* | Patrick Henry uttered the words, "Give me liberty or give me death." |
| | Crèvecoeur *Letters from an American Farmer* | |
| | Freneau *The Poems of Philip Freneau* | Declaration of Independence |
| | Equiano *The Interesting Narrative of the Life of Olaudah Equiano* | The Treaty of Paris ends the Revolutionary War |
| | | Shay's Rebellion |
| | Rowson *Charlotte: A Tale of Truth* | George Washington elected first president of the United States |
| | | Washington, D.C. established as U.S. capitol |
| **1771** | Franklin *Autobiography*, Part I | |
| **1773** | Warren *The Adulateur* | |
| | Wheatley, *Poems* | |
| **1776** | Warren *The Blockheads* | |
| **1789** | Brown *The Power of Sympathy* | |
| **1793** David *The Death of Marat* | Martha Ballard begins her diary | |
| | Brown *Wieland, or the Transformation* | |
| **1797** | | John Adams elected president |
| **1799** | Brown *Arthur Mervyn* | Death of George Washington |
| **1801** | | Jefferson elected president |

# Glossary of Terms

**anglophile** a person who admires the English

**antinomianism** literally "against the law;" a belief, which the Puritans considered heretical, that a Christian, once saved, is free of all moral and legal obligations

**Arminianism** a form of heresy that declared a person could earn grace through good works

**bicameral** having two houses, as in a legislature

**blank verse** a verse form that is comprised of unrhymed lines of five stressed syllables

**broadside** a large sheet of paper printed on one side, an inexpensive method of distributing songs, poems, and political opinions

**Calvinists** followers of John Calvin who believed in predestination, the idea that certain people were chosen for salvation and all others condemned to eternal damnation

**canon** a set of works that literary experts and historians have decided have value and recommend to be read by any educated individual

**capitalism** an economic system characterized by private ownership of property and a free market that determines the price of goods and services

**chattel** an item of moveable property

**congregationalist** relating to a group of Protestant churches who believe that each congregation should be self-governing

**covenant** a promise

**covenant of grace** the idea that anyone who truly tries to believe in God would be saved

**covenant of works** the idea that salvation could be gained through good works

**convention** an established technique or way of doing things

**crucible** a vessel that can be subjected to extremely high heat without breaking; can also mean a difficult test

**ecclesiastical** church related

**Elect** a term used by the Puritans to refer to someone who was predestined for salvation; also called Saints

**elegy** a poem or song of sorrow, composed to honor a person who has died

**Enlightenment** movement in the seventeenth century in which scientists and philosophers began to question religious authority and to see human reason as the ultimate tool in the discovery of truth

**entail** a method of limiting the inheritance of property to specified heirs with the purpose of keeping large holdings intact

**explicated** carefully analyzed word-by-word in order to craw out the true meaning of a text

**federal** anything based on the idea of promises or treaties

**genre** a category of artistic, musical, or literary composition characterized by a particular style, form, or content

**Great Migration** the period between 1620 and 1640 during which more than 20,000 Puritans arrived in America

**Great Spirit** Native American term for the Creator

**haiku** Japanese poem comprised of seventeen syllables

**heroic couplet** lines written in iambic pentameter—five stressed alternating with five unstressed beats—rhymed in pairs

**humanism** concept or philosophy based on the revival of classical studies and tending to emphasize secular concerns over spiritual ones

**indentured servants** typically young men who agreed to work for a landowner for a period of years in return for the price of passage to America

**introspection** looking inside oneself

**jeremiad** sermons delivered to alert parishioners to a minister's deep concern about the direction the congregation, village, or colony as a whole was taking; refers to the prophet Jeremiah and connotes a tale of sorrow or disappointment

**justification** a term used by Puritans to describe the conversion experience

**laissez faire** a doctrine opposing governmental interference in economic affairs

**manifest destiny** term used to justify and ennoble America's westward expansion

**matrilineal** tracing descent through the maternal line

**mercantile** having to do with merchants

**mercantilism** term coined by the Scottish economist Adam Smith, meaning the opposite of a free-market system

**metaphysical** reality beyond what can be perceived by the senses, a spiritual reality

**miscegenation** the mixture of races, especially by marriage

**misogyny** the hatred of women

**mnemonic** a memory aid

**pantheism** the idea that equates God with nature and natural forces

**participatory democracy** a form of government in which the people do not elect representatives but actually vote on each issue

**Protestant Reformation** a sixteenth-century religious movement that began as an attempt to reform the Roman Catholic Church but resulted in the development of Protestantism

**Puritan** a member of a group who wanted to purify the Church of England of any traces of Roman Catholicism

**representative democracy** a form of government in which the people elect representatives to vote on their behalf

**Saint** a Puritan term for someone predestined to be saved

**sanctification** a Puritan term that referred to behaving like a person who had experienced a true conversion

**self-conscious** in literature, a kind of writing that is focused on the literary art itself, that draws attention to the techniques used

**separatist** a member of a group who wanted to separate from the Church of England

**slave narrative** a firsthand account of slavery by someone who experienced it
**stereotype** a mental picture held in common a group and that represents an oversimplified idea or prejudiced attitude
**symbolic** representing something behind or beyond surface reality
**tariff** tax on goods from other nations
**tenet** doctrine
**theocracy** the government of a state by divine guidance
**Tory** term used to refer to those who were loyal to the British during the American Revolution
**typology** a belief that events in the New Testament were prefigured in the Old Testament; the study of the Bible based on these ideas

# Biographical Glossary

**Bailey, Abigail Abbott** (1746–1815) Memoirist who detailed her husband's incestuous relationship with their daughter. Bailey's memoirs were found with her possessions at the time of her death and were edited and published by her friend, Reverend Ethan Smith. During her 26 years of marriage to Asa Bailey, Abigail bore him 17 children. When she discovered that he was abusing their daughter, she asked him for a divorce. He agreed but tricked her into traveling to New York with him. He abandoned her there, thinking he was rid of her, but she traveled back to New Hampshire, by herself, on horseback. With the help of her brothers, she was able to divorce him.

**Barlow, Joel** (1754–1812) Author and member of the Connecticut Wits, also called the Hartford Wits. Joel Barlow was born in Redding, Connecticut in 1754. In 1787, Barlow published his epic, "The Vision of Columbus," a poem that made him an immediate celebrity. He traveled to France in 1788, where he witnessed the French Revolution. He also wrote on behalf of the Girondists, an anti-monarchist political party. He sailed to England in 1791 but left soon after because his pamphlet "Advice to the Privileged Orders" was banned by the British government. He returned to France, where he composed his most popular poem, the mock epic "Hasty Pudding" (1793). Barlow returned to America in 1805 and published an "enlarged" version of "The Vision of Columbus" (entitled "The Colombiad") in 1807. In 1811, Barlow returned to France as the U.S. minister to the French Court. Napoleon invited Barlow to meet him in Vilna, Poland, to witness the signing of a treaty, but when Barlow arrived, the French army was in the midst of its retreat from Russia. Barlow, traveling with the army, died from exposure and was buried in Poland.

**Ballard, Martha** (1735–1812) Diarist and midwife, who practiced in Hallowell, Maine. Ballard was born in Oxford, Massachusetts, in 1735, to Elijah Moore and Dorothy Learned Moore. She married Ephraim Ballard in 1754 and had seven children between 1756 and 1779. Three of her children died in a diphtheria epidemic in 1769. Martha began the diary for which she is now known at the age of 50 and wrote nearly every day until her death at the age of 67. As a midwife, she delivered more than 800 children during that period.

**Barton, Clara** (1821–1912) Founder of the American Red Cross. The great-great niece of Martha Ballard, Clara Barton was born Clarissa Harlowe Barton in Oxford, Massachusetts. She trained as a teacher and taught for many years, even founding a school in New Jersey. When the school's board passed her over for the director's position and offered the job to a man, she left in disgust and took a job as a clerk with the U.S. Patent Office. During the Civil War (1861–1865), Barton began to solicit donations of medical supplies for the soldiers and eventually got permission to work on the battlefields of Virginia treating wounded soldiers. During a European trip in 1868, Barton learned of the work of the Red Cross. She worked with that organization during the Franco-Prussian War (1870–1871). In 1881, she founded the American Red Cross and served as the organization's president until 1904.

**Bradford, William** (1590–1657) Governor of Plymouth Colony during its first 30 years. William Bradford was born in Yorkshire, England. He was orphaned as a young boy and lived with a variety of relatives. He attended his first Separatist church service at the age of 12, and by 17 was a church member. Separatists, people who had separated from the Church of England, were persecuted in England at the time, and in 1609 Bradford joined a group of separatists who migrated to the Netherlands in search of freedom of religion. Bradford was among those who organized a group of 100 pilgrims to undertake a journey to the "new world" in 1620. While still on board the *Mayflower* Bradford was among those who drafted the Mayflower Compact, a document signed by all the men aboard the ship in which they pledged to organized into a "civil Body Politick" and to live by the rule of law. In 1621 Bradford was chosen governor of the colony and was re-elected 30 times.

**Bradstreet, Anne Dudley** (c. 1612–1672) The first published poet in America. Anne Dudley was the daughter of Thomas Dudley, a Puritan, who served as chief steward to the Earl of Lincoln. As a girl, Bradstreet had access to the Earl's extensive library and took full advantage of the opportunity to read extensively. She married Simon Bradstreet at the age of 16 and left England two years later, with her husband and father, to settle in the Puritan colony at Massachusetts Bay. She raised eight children while both her father and husband served as governors of Massachusetts. She also wrote poetry, the first volume of which, *The Tenth Muse Lately Sprung Up in America* was published in England in 1650. Without her knowledge, her brother-in-law saw to the publication of this volume during a trip he took to England that year. She and her husband moved several times during their lives, each time to remote frontier areas where the family was in danger of attack or kidnapping by the Native American tribes nearby. Few details of Bradstreet's life, other than that which is revealed in her poetry, are known.

**Columbus, Christopher** (1451–1506) Explorer who is credited with the discovery of America. Columbus was born in Genoa, Italy, the son of a weaver. His seafaring life began at the age of 14. In 1476, he arrived in Lisbon, Portugal, after having escaped from a burning ship. There he married Felipa Perestrello e Monez, whose father was a sea captain. He spent many years seeking financing for his dream of finding a sea route to India, until, in 1492, he was able to persuade Ferdinand and Isabella of Spain to finance the expedition. Columbus arrived in San Salvador in the Bahamas on October 12, 1492 and he promptly claimed the land for Spain. He left 38 men behind and returned to Spain, where he was welcomed as a hero. Columbus's second voyage was a much larger expedition than the first, but it was unsuccessful and very disappointing to the explorer. All the men he had left in San Salvador had been massacred, he quarreled with his associates, and he suffered a grave illness. He returned to Spain in 1496. On his third voyage, Columbus discovered the South American mainland. During his final voyage from 1502–1504, Columbus sailed along the southern end of the Gulf of Mexico, vainly looking for a passage to India. Columbus died in Valladolid Spain in 1506, a disappointed man. Neither he nor anyone else at the time realized the magnitude of his discovery.

**Crèvecoeur, Hector St. John de** (1735–1813) Author of *Letters of an American Farmer.* Crèvecoeur was born in Normandy, France, and was educated in England. He came to America in 1754 and may have served under the British general, Montcalm, in Canada. After traveling around the Great Lakes region and throughout the Ohio valley, Crèvecoeur settled in Orange County, New York, where he wrote the work for which he is remembered today. His portrait of life in America is credited with persuading more than 500 families to leave France and settle in America. During the Revolutionary War, Crèvecoeur remained loyal to the British cause, and his farm was often attacked by American troops and Native Americans who fought on the side of the rebels. In 1780, on his way to France, he was captured in New York City and held as a spy for three months. He finally reached France in 1782, and he is credited for introducing the American potato there. Crèvecoeur returned to America in 1783, as French consul to the United States. He went in search of his family only to discover that his farm had been destroyed and that his wife had died only shortly before his arrival. In 1790, Crèvecoeur returned to France, where he died in 1813.

**Edwards, Jonathan** (1703–1758) One of the greatest American preachers and theologians of American Calvinism, and the third president of Princeton College. Johnathan Edwards was born in East Windsor, Connecticut, the only boy of eleven children born to Timothy Edwards, pastor of the Church at Northampton. Edwards entered Yale College at the age of 13, graduating four years later at the top of his class. In 1727, Edwards married Sarah Pierrepont, a deeply religious, even mystical woman. Together, they had eleven children. In 1728, Edwards became pastor at Northampton where his preaching helped to begin the religious revival known as the first Great Awakening. By 1748, however, Edwards's insistence on administering communion only to those who showed evidence of a true conversion had angered many members of his congregation, and he was dismissed from his church in 1750. Edwards then served as a missionary to the Housatonic Indians in Stockbridge, Massachusetts. As the most important theologian of his day, he was a natural choice for the presidency of Princeton College, to which position he was appointed in 1757, succeeding his son-in-law Aaron Burr, who had recently died. Burr, who was married to Edwards's daughter Esther, was the father of Aaron Burr, second vice president of the United States. Edwards's stint at Princeton was brief; he died six months after his appointment as a result of a smallpox inoculation.

**Foster, Hannah Webster** (1758–1840) Author of best-selling novel, *The Coquette: Or the History of Eliza Wharton* (1797), the first novel written by a native-born American woman. Foster was born in Salisbury, Massachusetts, the daughter of a wealthy merchant. Foster's mother died when she was very young, and her father sent her to boarding school, an experience that she wrote about in her second novel, *The Boarding School* (1799). After she left school, she moved to Boston where she wrote for local newspapers. In 1785, Foster married the Reverend John Foster, pastor of the First Parish Church in Brighton, Massachusetts. Her novel, *The Coquette,* written after the birth of her sixth and last child, was an astounding success; by 1840, it had gone through 30 editions. After publishing her second novel, *The Boarding School,* Foster returned to writing for newspapers. After the death of her husband in 1829, Foster moved to Montreal, Canada, to be near her two married daughters. She died there in 1840.

**Equiano, Olaudah** (c. 1745–1797) Also known as Gustavas Vassa, Equiano is known for his autobiography, which provides a first-hand account of the life of a slave in the eighteenth century. Equiano was born in what is now Nigeria, the son of a chief. At the age of ten or eleven, he and his sister were kidnapped and sold into slavery. Eventually, Equiano was bought by Michael Pascal, an officer in the British Navy. Accompanying Pascal, Equiano traveled all over the world and learned to read and write. He fought alongside Pascal in the Seven Years War between Britain and France. After the war, Pascal sold Equiano to a sea captain, who sold him to Robert King, a Quaker in Monserrat, West Indies. Here Equiano witnessed slavery at its most cruel. He was eventually able to buy his freedom, and he returned to England. He worked for a time as a hairdresser but eventually went back to sea, joining Captain John Phipps on a voyage to find a passage to India across the North Pole. On this trip, one of his crew mates was Horatio Nelson, who would eventually become one of England's greatest naval heroes. On his return to England, Equiano converted to Christianity and began to campaign against the institution of slavery. In 1789, he wrote his autobiography, *The Interesting Narrative of the Life of Olaudah Equiano.* He married an Englishwoman, Susanna Cullen, in 1792, and together they had two daughters. Equiano died in 1797, ten years before the slave trade was abolished in England.

**Franklin, Benjamin** (1706–1790) Writer, inventor, diplomat, philanthropist, and the model for many American rags-to-riches stories. Born in Boston in 1706, Benjamin Franklin was one of seventeen children of Josiah Franklin, a soap maker. When Franklin was 15, he was apprenticed to his brother James, who printed a newspaper called *The New England Courant.* Franklin and his brother quarreled frequently, and Franklin eventually decided to run away. After a harrowing journey he arrived, penniless, in Philadelphia on October 6, 1723. On his first day there, he met Deborah Read, the woman who would become his wife. Franklin made his fortune through hard work and dedication. He published a newspaper, an almanac, and was involved in a variety of civic improvements, including founding a library, a philosophical society, a hospital, a volunteer fire department, and an insurance society. He was also an inventor, credited with important discoveries about electricity and practical inventions such as a stove and bifocals. In the 1760s and 1770s Franklin was an active supporter of the American Revolution. He was elected to the Second Continental Congress and was one of five who wrote the Declaration of Independence. He served as America's ambassador to France during the Revolutionary War. Since the help of the French was crucial for American victory, Franklin's intervention there was of immeasurable importance to the American victory. After the war, Franklin served as a delegate to the Constitutional Convention and was one of the signers of the Constitution. He died at the age of 84; so famous was he that 20,000 people attended his funeral.

**Franks, Abigaill Levy** (1696–1756) Collected letters reveal much about colonial life and family. Neither birth nor death records exist for Abigaill Levy Franks, although the years of her birth and death are known. She was born in London, England, in 1696 and came to New York City with her parents in 1703. She was the only girl of five children. Abigaill's mother, Richea, died when she was eleven, leaving her to care for her father and brothers. Her father, Moses, remarried and had seven more children with his second wife, Grace Mears. Franks disliked her stepmother, which may have been one of the reasons that she married at the relatively young age of 16 to Isaac Franks, an associate of her father. Her marriage was a good one, and she and Isaac had nine children, two of whom died young. Franks is best known today for her letters to her oldest son, Napthali, sent between the years 1733 and 1748. Napthali left home for London at the age of 17 and never returned. The circumstances of Franks's death are not known, but her husband outlived her by a decade.

**Freneau, Philip** (1752–1832) Poet of the American Revolution and the fledgling democracy. Freneau was born in New York City to a French father and a Scottish mother. He intended to study for the ministry when he entered the College at Nassau, later Princeton, but he turned to literature in the politically charged atmosphere of pre-Revolutionary-War Princeton. During this time Freneau wrote "The Power of Fancy," a poem about the power of the imagination, as well as many satirical and witty pieces. Inspired by patriotism, Freneau, along with Hugh Henry Brackenridge, wrote an epic poem entitled "The Rising Glory of America," which Brackenridge read at their commencement. Freneau could not earn a living as a writer, so he took various jobs to support himself while he wrote satires against the British during the Revolution. By 1790 he had published two collections of poetry, married, and taken a job as an editor in New York. His friends, Thomas Jefferson and James Madison, however, persuaded him to leave that position and to publish a newspaper in Philadelphia that reflected Jefferson's political views. Thus Freneau's *National Gazette* came into being. Freneau died in Monmouth County, New Jersey, in 1832.

**Henry, Patrick** (1736–1799) American orator and patriot. Patrick Henry was born in Hanover County, Virginia, the son of John and Sarah Winston Henry. He tried out several professions unsuccessfully before he settled on the law, which he studied on his own. He made a name for himself as a lawyer by arguing the Parson's Cause, a case which resulted from King George's arbitrarily overturning a Virginia law. His work on this case made him an instant celebrity in Virginia. In a speech attacking the infamous Stamp Act in 1765, Henry uttered the famous words, "If this be treason, make the most of it." He delivered his best remembered oration in 1775 at the second Virginia Convention. "I know not what course others may take, but as for me, give me liberty or give me death" became the cry that led the colonies to revolution. During the war Henry served as the first governor of the state of Virginia; he was elected to three consecutive terms. Henry originally opposed the U.S. Constitution because he feared it invested too much power in the central government and took away power from the states and the people. However, he agreed to vote to ratify the constitution after a Bill of Rights was added. Henry married twice and fathered fifteen children. He died in Red Hill, Virginia, in 1799.

**Hutchinson, Anne Marbury** (1591–1643) Anne Marbury was born in Lincolnshire, England, the daughter of a Puritan minister. She married William Hutchinson in 1612. The couple and their 15 children migrated to Massachusetts in 1634, when Hutchinson was 43. Upon arrival in the colony, Hutchinson began the practice of having neighbor women come to her house for prayer and religious discussion. Soon, men began to attend these discussion groups, and Hutchinson's opinion began to be taken seriously. The idea of a woman as a religious leader frightened some, including John Winthrop, governor of the colony. She was eventually brought to trial and convicted of heresy for her religious ideas. She and some of her followers left Massachusetts in 1636 and established a settlement in what is now Rhode Island. After her husband's death in 1642, Hutchinson moved to Pelham Bay on Long Island Sound, where she and five of her children were massacred by Mohicans.

**Jefferson, Thomas** (1743–1826) Second President of the United States, principal author of the Declaration of Independence. Jefferson was born in Albemarle County Virginia. His father, Peter, was a landowner and his mother, Jane Randolph, was a member of one of Virginia's most prominent families. Jefferson attended the College of William and Mary and, upon graduation, studied law. He was elected to the Virginia House of Burgesses in 1769 and served there for six years. He married Martha Wayles Skelton in 1772; the couple had six children, only two of whom lived to adulthood. Jefferson came to national attention in 1774, when he wrote a pamphlet arguing that "The God who gave us life gave us liberty at the same time" and that a free people did not owe allegiance to a king. Jefferson was elected to the Second Continental Congress in 1776, and was chosen as one of five to write the Declaration of Independence. From 1776 to 1779 Jefferson served in the Virginia House of Delegates, and in 1779, he was elected Governor of Virginia. From 1785–1789, Jefferson was U.S. minister to France. He was named Secretary of State in the administration of George Washington, and he served in that post until 1793. He was vice-president to John Adams and was elected to the presidency in 1800. In 1803 he presided over the Louisiana Purchase, which doubled the size of the United States. In 1819, Jefferson founded the University of Virginia. He died on July 4, 1826, the 50th anniversary of the signing of the Declaration of Independence.

**Mather, Cotton** (1663–1728) Among the most famous of the New England Puritans, a clergyman and prolific writer. Cotton Mather came from one of the most distinguished families in New England. His father was the Rev. Increase Mather, President of Harvard, and his grandfathers, John Cotton and Richard Mather, were well-known Puritan clergymen. Mather entered Harvard College at the tender age of 12 and received a master's degree at the age of 18. He was ordained as a minister in 1685 and worked with his father's congregation at the North Church in Boston, becoming pastor there at his father's death in 1723. He is remembered today for his prodigious literary output—more than 450 books and pamphlets—including *Essays to Do Good* (1710), *Christian Philsospher* (1721), and his masterpiece, *Magnalia Christi Americana* (1702), a history of New England from its founding to his own time. He is also, unfortunately, remembered for his involvement in the Salem witchcraft trials. Mather believed that the devil was tempting the people of New England, and he hoped that the evidence of this he saw in the outbreak in Salem would lead people to a renewal of faith. But the episode had the opposite effect, weakening the power of the Puritan clergy in New England. Mather married three times and had fifteen children. When he died in 1728, only his third wife and one child survived him.

**Paine, Thomas** (1737–1809) Author of *Common Sense, The Rights of Man,* and *The Age of Reason.* Paine was born in Thetford, England. He did not do well in school, so he was apprenticed to his father, who made corsets. At the age of 19, he went to sea briefly, then took a position as a tax officer. In 1774 Paine met Benjamin Franklin, who helped Paine to immigrate to Philadelphia. Once there, Paine worked as a journalist and, in 1776, published his famous pamphlet, *Common Sense,* an impassioned defense of the idea of American Independence. He joined the Continental Army and continued to have great success with his writing. His series of pamphlets printed as *The Crisis* (1776–1783) was read by a larger percentage of the American population of the day than the percentage of today's population that watches the Superbowl. After the war, Paine returned to England, where he wrote *The Rights of Man* (1792), a work in praise of the French Revolution that nearly got him arrested because of its anti-monarchism. He escaped to France where he was arrested and imprisoned in 1793 for opposing the execution of Louis XVI. While in prison, he wrote *The Age of Reason* (1796), a book many felt was anti-Christian. Paine was freed, barely escaping execution, through the help of James Monroe, then U.S. Minister to France. Paine returned to America in 1802, only to find that most Americans now regarded him as the "atheist" author of *The Age of Reason* rather than the patriot who had penned *Common Sense.* Paine died in New York in 1809.

**Smith, Captain John** (1580–1631) Explorer and historian. John Smith was born in Willoughby, England. He was apprenticed to a merchant but, upon his father's death in 1596, left England in search of adventure. After traveling throughout Europe and northern Asia, Smith returned to England in 1605. Still restless, he joined an expedition to the New World, arriving in Jamestown, Virginia, in 1607. There, he continued his explorations, mapping the Chesapeake Bay region. Smith returned to England in 1609 as a result of a severe burn he received when his gunpowder caught fire. He returned to America in 1614 and explored extensively in Maine and Massachusetts, an area he named "New England." Smith died in England in 1631.

**Taylor, Edward** (1642–1729) Poet. Taylor was born in Leicestershire, England. As a Puritan, he may have been unable to find work after the Restoration of Charles II to the throne of England, leading him to immigrate to New England in 1668. He attended Harvard, graduating within three years, and became a minister in the town of Westfield, Massachusetts. This was a frontier town, and Taylor called his congregation to worship by beating a drum. While he served his congregation, he also wrote poetry. Most of what he wrote was not published until the late 1930s after Thomas Johnson discovered the manuscript in the Yale University Library. His most famous work is *Preparatory Meditations before my Approach to the Lords Supper,* a series of 217 long devotional poems Taylor wrote to help him prepare to take communion. Taylor died in 1729.

**Washington, George** (1732–1799) Revolutionary War general and first President of the United States. George Washington was born in Virginia, the oldest son of Augustine Washington and his second wife, Mary Ball Washington. Upon the death of his father in 1743, the young Washington went to live with his half-brother Lawrence on his estate at Mount Vernon. Washington began work as a surveyor in 1748, surveying lands in the Shenandoah Valley. During the French and Indian War (1754–63) Washington's heroism resulted in his being promoted to lieutenant colonel by the age of 22. At 23, he was made a full colonel and commander-in-chief of the Virginia militia. Washington inherited Mount Vernon when Lawrence died, and he returned there in 1758 to farm and pursue his interest in politics. He married Martha Dandridge Custis, a wealthy widow, in 1759 and was elected to the Virginia House of Burgesses the same year. Over the years, he spoke out repeatedly against the British and was especially opposed to land policies that prevented westward expansion. He attended both the first and second Continental Congresses in 1774 and 1775, and, in June of 1775, he was made commander-in-chief of the Continental army. After the war, Washington returned to Mount Vernon. In 1789, he was unanimously elected to the presidency of the newly formed United States of America. After leaving office in 1797, Washington again retired to Mount Vernon, where he died in 1799.

**Wheatley, Phillis** (1753–1784) America's first black poet. Phillis Wheatley was born in Senegal, Africa. She was taken as a slave and brought to Boston in 1761. There, she was purchased by John Wheatley as a servant for his wife Susannah. The Wheatleys treated the young girl as almost a member of the family, and their daughter, Mary, was assigned to tutor her. She learned not only English with remarkable speed but also Greek and Latin. She began to write poetry in her early teens. Her talent gained her wide recognition when she wrote a poem on the death of the evangelical preacher George Whitefield. In 1773, a volume of her poetry, *Poems on Various Subjects, Religious and Moral,* was published in England; in the same year, John Wheatley freed her. In 1778, Wheatley married John Peters and they had three children. Peters later abandoned her and the children, and Wheatley was forced to work as a servant to support her family. She died, impoverished, in 1784.

**Williams, Roger** (c. 1600–1683) Founder of Rhode Island. Roger Williams was born in England between 1600 and 1603. He graduated from Cambridge University in 1627; two years later he married Mary Barnard. The couple immigrated to Massachusetts in 1630, arriving in Boston in 1631. They had six children, all born in America. Williams preached at churches in Salem and Plymouth, Massachusetts, but his religious and political ideas so angered the Puritan leaders that they sought to deport him back to England. Williams escaped from Massachusetts and eventually settled near Naragansett Bay, in what is now Rhode Island. One of Williams's unpopular ideas as far as the Puritans were concerned was that he believed Native Americans should be fairly compensated for their land. Thus, when he settled in Rhode Island, he purchased the land for a fair price from the owners. He named his settlement Providence, as a way of giving thanks to God, and he declared his new colony to be a place where all religions could be practiced freely. Williams traveled to England in 1643 to obtain a charter for his new colony. During this voyage, he wrote his best-known work, *Key to the Languages of America.* Williams served as Rhode Island's governor from 1654 to 1658. He died in Providence in 1683.

**Winthrop, John** (1587–1649) First governor of Massachusetts. John Winthrop was born in Suffolk, England, the only son of Adam Winthrop a well-to-do landowner and his wife, Anne Browne Winthrop. He studied for two years at Trinity College, Cambridge, and then returned home to learn how to manage his father's estate. In his thirties, Winthrop converted to the Puritan faith. When, in 1630, members of the Massachusetts Bay Company decided to immigrate to New England, they chose Winthrop as their leader. By this time Winthrop had six children and had been twice widowed. When he departed for Massachusetts, he left his third wife, Margaret, in England because she was expecting a child. In 1631, Margaret joined Winthrop; with her he had eight children. She died in 1647, and Winthrop remarried the next year. With his fourth wife, he had one son. During the early years of the colony, Winthrop spent a great deal of his own money to make the enterprise a success, literally feeding many of the colonists from the profits of the sale of his estate. He was chosen as governor of Massachusetts twelve times, dying in office in 1649. His *History of New England* (1825–26) is an invaluable chronicle of the growth of the colony and of the period in general.

# Further Reading


### Chapter 1. The First 300 Years

**Erdoes, Richard,** and Alfonso Ortiz, eds. *American Indian Myths and Legends.* New York: Pantheon, 1984.

**Philip, Neil,** ed. *Earth Always Endures: Native American Poems.* New York: Viking, 1996.

### Chapter 2. The Literature of Puritanism

*Africans in America: The Terrible Transformation.* <http://www.pbs.org/wgbh/aia/part1/narrative/html>

**Carey, Brycchan,** Markman Ellis, Sara Salih, eds. *Discourses of Slavery and Abolition: Britain and Its Colonies, 1760–1838: An Anthology of Critical Essays.* UK: Palgrave Macmillan, 2004.

### Chapter 3. Aspects of Colonial American Culture

**Appleby, Joyce O.** *Inheriting the Revolution: The First Generation of Americans.* Cambridge: Harvard University Press, 2000.

**Gaustad, Edwin,** and Leigh Schmidt. *The Religious History of America.* New York: HarperCollins, 2002.

**Heimert, Alan,** and Andrew Delbanco, eds. *The Puritans in America: A Narrative Anthology.* Cambridge: Harvard University Press, 1985; rpt. 2001.

**Miller, Perry.** *Errand into the Wilderness.* Cambridge: Harvard University Press, 1956; rpt. 1996.

________. *The New England Mind: From Colony to Province.* Cambridge: Harvard University Press, 1953.

________. *The New England Mind: The Seventeenth Century.* Cambridge: Harvard University Press, 1939.

### Chapter 4. The Literature of the American Enlightenment

**Lawrence, D. H.** *Studies in Classic American Literature.* London: Penguin, 1923; rpt. New York: Penguin, 1977.

**Lewis, R. W. B.** *The American Adam: Innocence, Tragedy, and Tradition in the Nineteenth Century.* Chicago: University of Chicago Press, 1955; rpt. 2001.

**Miller, Perry.** *Nature's Nation.* New York: Belknap Press, 1967.

### Chapter 5. The Literature of the American Revolution

**Silverman, Kenneth.** *A Cultural History of the American Revolution.* New York: Thomas Y. Crowell, 1976.

**Taylor, Alan.** *American Colonies: The Settling of North America.* N.Y. and London: Penguin, 2001.

*Thomas Jefferson Digital Archive.* <http://etext.lib/virginia.edu/jefferson/>

### Chapter 6. Literary and Cultural Visions of the New Nation

**Eliott, Emory.** *The Cambridge Introduction to Early American Literature.* Cambridge: Cambridge University Press, 2002.

**Homberger, Eric,** *American Writers and Radical Politics, 1900–39.* New York: St. Martins Press, 1986.

**Irving, Katrina.** *Immigrant Mothers.* Urbana, IL: University of Illinois Press, 2000.

**Rideout, Walter.** *The Radical Novel in the United States 1900–1954.* Cambridge: Harvard University Press, 1956.

**Ziff, Larzer.** *The American 1890's: Life and Times of a Lost Generation.* New York: Viking Press, 1966.

### Chapter 7. Women's Voices

**Berkin, Carol.** *First Generations: Women in Colonial America*. New York: Hill and Wang, 1997.

**Collins, Gale.** *America's Women: 400 Years of Dolls, Drudges, Helpmates, and Heroines*. New York: Harper Perennial, 2007.

**Cully, Margo.** *A Day at a Time: The Diary Literature of American Women Writers, From 1764 to the Present*. New York: The Feminist Press at CUNY, 1993.

**Gelles, Edith B.,** ed., *The Letters of Abigaill Levy Franks, 1733–1748.* New Haven and London: Yale University Press, 2004.

**Ulrich, Laurel Thatcher.** *A Midwife's Tale: The Life of Martha Ballard Based on Her Diary, 1785–1812.* New York: Vintage, 1991. <http://dohistory.org>

# Index